On the Philosophy of Mind

On the Philosophy of Mind

Barbara Montero
The City University of New York Graduate Center

Australia • Brazil • Japan • Korea • Mexico • Singapore • Spain • United Kingdom • United States

WADSWORTH
CENGAGE Learning

On the Philosophy of Mind

Barbara Montero

Executive Editor: Marcus Boggs

Acquisitions Editor: Worth Hawes

Assistant Editor: Sarah Perkins

Editorial Assistant: Daniel Vivacqua

Marketing Manager: Christina Shea

Marketing Assistant: Mary Anne Payumo

Marketing Communications Manager: Darlene Amidon-Brent

Project Manager, Editorial Production: Samen Iqbal

Creative Director: Rob Hugel

Art Director: Maria Epes

Print Buyer: Linda Hsu

Permissions Editor: Roberta Broyer

Production Service: Tintu Thomas Integra

Copy Editor: Linda Ireland

Compositor: Integra

For product information and technology assistance, contact us at
Cengage Learning Customer & Sales Support, 1-800-354-9706.
For permission to use material from this text or product, submit all requests online at
cengage.com/permissions.
Further permissions questions can be e-mailed to **permissionrequest@cengage.com.**

Library of Congress Control Number: 2008920400

Student Edition:
ISBN-13: 978-0-495-00502-5
ISBN-10: 0-495-00502-9

Wadsworth
10 Davis Drive
Belmont, CA 94002-3098
USA

Cengage Learning is a leading provider of customized learning solutions with office locations around the globe, including Singapore, the United Kingdom, Australia, Mexico, Brazil, and Japan. Locate your local office at **international.cengage.com/region.**

Cengage Learning products are represented in Canada by Nelson Education, Ltd.

For your course and learning solutions, visit **academic.cengage.com.**

Purchase any of our products at your local college store or at our preferred online store **www.ichapters.com.**

Printed in the United States of America
1 2 3 4 5 6 7 12 11 10 09 08

Contents

CONTENTS

1

Philosophy of Mind: Introduction

Philosophy is to be studied, not for the sake of any definite answers to its questions, since no definite answers can, as a rule, be known to be true, but rather for the sake of the questions themselves; because these questions enlarge our conception of what is possible, enrich our intellectual imagination and diminish the dogmatic assurance which closes the mind against speculation; but above all because, through the greatness of the universe which philosophy contemplates, the mind also is rendered great, and becomes capable of that union which constitutes its highest good.
—BERTRAND RUSSELL (1912)

The proper method of philosophy consists in clearly conceiving the insoluble problems in all their insolubility and then in simply contemplating them, fixedly and tirelessly, year after year, without any hope, patiently waiting.
—SIMONE WEIL (1943)

Have you ever wondered whether other people see colors the way you do? Perhaps when you look at newly sprouted grass, it looks to you the way ripe tomatoes look to me. But if it does, how could I ever know that it does? We could both take tests that are used to identify color blindness and that would require us to do such things as identify numerals written in red on a background of green. But this would not resolve the issue, since it could be that when you see the red numeral two, you see the same color I see when I look at grass, but you have just learned to call that color "red." If only I could jump into your skin and find out what your experience of the numeral was like, then I would know whether you see the color red the way I do. But since that is impossible and since there seems to be no test that could reveal an answer, it seems that we are left with an irresolvable mystery.

Here is another puzzle that at some time or another may have crossed your mind. The cells that make up your body are constantly dying off and being replaced. Although the cells that die in the brain are replaced infrequently, if at all, they are constantly being reorganized. Yet despite all this change, you do not turn into a different person. Yes, your personality has developed and changed quite a bit since you were born, as has your body, but nonetheless every moment of your life you have still been you; it is *you* who has changed. But what is it that makes you the same individual throughout your life despite all the changes? It seems that if the physical material of your brain and body is constantly changing, it has to be something other than your brain and body that makes you who you are. But what could this be? We seem to think that our brains are especially important in creating our identity, in making us who we are. But perhaps it is not the brain itself that is relevant to your being you, but rather what the brain does, such as make us think, remember, have sensations and emotions, and so forth, that is the key factor in determining who you are. Could all the information in your brain, such as your memories and knowledge, be stored in a computer so that after you die, it could be programmed into someone else, making that someone else *you*? Or would your having a different body and brain turn you into a different person entirely? If you think it wouldn't, what are the sorts of changes that you could undergo that would turn you into a different person?

Perhaps the question that provokes more curiosity than any other question about the mind is, "What is to become of us after our bodily death?" When your brain stops functioning does that mean that you no longer exist? And if you no longer exist when your brain stops functioning, what does this show? Does it show that when you are alive you are nothing more than a functioning physical brain and body? It certainly suggests this view. However, couldn't it be that you also have a soul that ceases to exist when your brain and body cease to function? Perhaps you think that there is an afterlife and that your soul will still exist even when your brain and body no longer function. But where is the soul when we are alive? Many think that human beings are compilations of immaterial souls and human bodies. Although it is clear where the human body is, it is not at all clear where the soul is. Is it spatially located inside of the body, perhaps in the brain? If it is, why have we never seen it? If not, where would it be? And wherever it is, how is it connected to its bearer? Moreover, what is it about this immaterial thing "the soul" that makes it different from other souls and makes it you?

If you have pondered any of these questions before then this book is for you. The central topic is the philosophy of mind, which is the philosophical investigation into the nature of the mind, the soul, and what it is to be a human being. The mind has been an important area of philosophical inquiry since the first philosopher in the Western tradition attempted to explain the animating principle in nature in terms of mind or soul. And today, not only is philosophy of mind a central area of study and research in and of itself, but philosophical questions about the mind also come up in almost all branches of philosophy and infiltrate a variety of disciplines outside of philosophy, including psychology, neuroscience, economics, evolutionary biology, and linguistics.

The main goal of this book is to provide an introduction to some of the central problems in philosophy of mind. We will delve extensively into the relationship between mind and body. We will also address questions about the nature of consciousness, thought and emotions, the idea that computers can think, the possibility of free will, and immortality. I will not be providing definitive answers to the questions raised in this book. And indeed, after rejecting one solution after another to various philosophical puzzles, as at times I will do, you will probably want to ask, "But what *is* the answer?" Or at least you might want me to tell you what I think the answer is. Although I will sometimes lead you through my reasoning for thinking that certain responses fail to answer a given question, typically I will not present solutions to the problems we will be investigating, for philosophical questions are rarely answered in any definitive way. This is not because philosophical questions have no solutions. They do; or at least, philosophers often think that they do. Rather, it is because the answers to philosophical questions often lie just beyond our reach. Indeed, some philosophers define a philosophical question as one that the human mind is able to understand and finds compelling yet not even in principle is able to answer. This does not mean that philosophy is just about tying oneself in knots trying to figure out paradoxes, such as whether there is an exception to the rule that states every rule has an exception (though there is a place for thinking about paradoxes like these as well). Rather, it is thought that in searching for the answers to these unanswerable questions we will come closer to finding the truth and to understanding deep and important questions. This is the nature of philosophy: One finds rewards in the process, but not always in the final product.

I like to think that the practice of philosophy is similar to the practice of ballet. Both philosophy and ballet aim at an ideal that is for the most part unattainable. In ballet, this ideal involves such things as standing in the perfect fifth position, landing from a jump with the utmost elasticity, and executing the most difficult move with consummate grace—achievements that are, for most part, physically impossible. In philosophy, this ideal involves finding solutions to the great philosophical puzzles, puzzles that philosophers have been trying to solve for centuries—an achievement that is, for the most part, mentally impossible.

So be prepared to struggle with the ideas you will encounter in this book. If you persevere, your toils will be rewarded. I have heard it said that when college students are asked which class they are currently taking that they would most like to drop, the most common answer is philosophy. Many years later, however, when asked which class they benefited from the most, the most common answer is . . . you've guessed it: again, philosophy.

We have now completed our warm-up; let us begin to exercise and stretch, not the body, but the mind.

SUGGESTIONS FOR FURTHER READING

For a general introduction to the philosophical process, Bertrand Russell's essay "The Value of Philosophy," in his short work *The Problems of Philosophy* (1912), is quite inspiring. For a more specific introduction to philosophy of mind, *The Mind's I: Fantasies and Reflections on Self & Soul,* edited by Douglas Hofstader and Daniel Dennett, is designed to be accessible and intriguing to those with little or no philosophical background.

2

The Mind-Body Problem

Ah! my poor brain is racked and crazed,
My spirit and senses amazed!
—JOHANN WOLFGANG VON GOETHE,
FAUST (1808)

It's impossible I should have a mind and I have one.
—SAMUEL BECKETT, "FIZZLE 3" (1976)

The other day, while I was happily ensconced behind a pile of
books at the New York Public Library, the image of being
imprisoned flashed before my mind, which was followed, naturally,
by a sudden, strong desire to escape. It was spring and the sky was
clear, so after deliberating a bit over whether the benefit I would reap
from some fresh air would be worth the cost of the time it would take
to get some, I set off and soon found myself in Central Park. The
sight of tulips blooming red, purple, yellow, pink, the warmth of the
sun on my skin, and the brisk walk revitalized mind and body. I
returned to the library content. My initial happiness, the image that
crossed my mind of being imprisoned, my pressing desire to go
outside, the processes of deliberating whether to go, my experience
of seeing the colored tulips, my feeling the warmth of the sun, and
my contentment afterward were all part of the furniture of my mental
life. All these processes occurred, in some sense, in my mind. But
what makes these processes mental processes? What is it that sets apart
processes, such as sensation, emotion, thought, and desire, from other

5

processes occurring in us, such as respiration, circulation, digestion, and growth? Or more generally, what is this thing we call "the mind"?

Our minds are our constant companions. Our mental lives begin in the womb and pause (or at least slow down significantly) only during dreamless sleep or coma. When we think, desire, feel, emote, or believe, we are using our minds. We know that the workings of the mind are intimately connected to the workings of the brain. We know, for example, that damage to the primary visual areas of the occipital lobe in the brain causes blindness and that damage to the boundary of the temporal and parietal lobes of the brain can render individuals unable to comprehend spoken language. But how are the workings of gray matter relevant to my visual experience of the radiant array of colors I see before my eyes? How could electrical impulses in certain areas of the brain account for my understanding a line of poetry or even my son's request for a glass of milk? How can the mechanistic brain give rise to flowing conscious experience? The mystery of how this happens seems, as the English biologist Julian Huxley put it, just as perplexing as the mystery of how the Djin emanates from Aladdin's lamp. To solve this mystery is to solve the venerable mind-body problem, a problem philosophers have been struggling with for thousands of years.

Although philosophers may not have come up with the solution to the mind-body problem over these thousands of years, they have made great strides in understanding and clarifying the panoply of possible solutions to it. These potential solutions tell us how the mind and body could be aligned. For example, one possible solution to the problem is to say that mental processes are nothing more than certain neural processes: Visual experience is nothing more than properly functioning neural activity in the primary visual areas of the occipital lobe, understanding spoken language is just neural activity at the boundary of the temporal and parietal lobes, and so on.

Another line of reasoning leads to the view that there is a causal relation between mind and brain. On this view, for example, activity in the visual cortex *causes* sight. And still another view is that mind and brain have no causal interaction at all, for example, that neural processes and visual experience merely run along parallel tracks, each perfectly correlated with the other yet proceeding in complete causal isolation from the other. Some even hold that experience itself doesn't exist and that somehow all our mental life is an elaborate grand illusion. Although each of these views has its champions, there

6

is no agreement about which view is best, or most likely to be correct. Our minds are our most precious commodities, yet we know so little about how they fit into the physical world.

But do we even know that the mind does fit into the physical world? Sometimes the mind-body problem is thought of as the problem of specifying how the mind fits into the physical world. To put it this way assumes, however, that it does fit in and the problem is just to specify how it fits in. But as there are those who think that the mind is not physical (because, for example, it is your soul), the formulation of the mind-body problem should really be stated more neutrally. And a good neutral formulation is this:

> The mind-body problem: the problem of specifying the relationship between mind and body.

Typically, the brain is considered to be the aspect of body that is where all the action is. So often we can think of the mind-body problem as the problem of specifying the relationship between the mind and the brain or between mental properties (such as having a visual experience) and neural properties (such as having activity in the visual cortex). Specifying relationship between mind and brain is something science has not accomplished. Indeed, some philosophers think that although science can tell us what areas of the brain are correlated with various mental processes, science will never and perhaps even in principle could never tell us how the mind and brain are related. These philosophers typically see the mind as something you can understand only from a first-person point of view. That is, they think that you can understand the mind only by having a mind, while science, as they see it, investigates the world from a third-person point of view, by theory and observation. A cardiologist can perfectly understand what would happen to her heart if she were struck by lightning. And a neurologist can perfectly understand what goes on in the brain when we experience fear or elation (not now, but presumably in the future when neuroscience has progressed). But although a neuroscientist can understand what is happening in your brain when you experience fear, she cannot experience your fear. Only you, it seems, can do that.

What science reveals is one thing, but what we understand from the inside, from having experiences, is something else entirely. Why is this? Why can't science tell us about our inner lives? If it is true that science cannot tell us about our inner lives, the answer to this question must have something to do with the nature of science. Some philosophers think that it is precisely because of the limitations on what science can tell us that the mind-body problem is such a mystery. Science, these philosophers claim, tells us about the causal structure of the world. It tells us, for example, about what happens when electrons interact with neighboring nuclei to cause chemical bonding or about the interaction between living and nonliving components of an ecosystem. All these features of the world are relational, that is, they involve relations between things. But conscious experience seems to be part something that cannot be entirely captured in a description of its causes and effects. It is what philosophers call an "intrinsic" feature of the world, whereas science tells us only about that which is extrinsic.

Saying that science has not revealed whether mind and brain are one and the same thing is a bit misleading, since no one actually thinks that the mind is the entire brain. The brain is responsible for a number of functions, such as regulating heart rate and breathing, that do not pertain to the mind at all. So we need not ask whether the mind is just the brain: We already know that the mind is not the same thing as the brain, since not every aspect of the brain is relevant to the mind. Rather, the brain controls both mental and nonmental bodily functions. But some aspects of the brain are relevant to the workings of the mind, such as your desire to go outside, your experience of color and of warmth on your skin. The appropriate question to ask, then, is whether the mind is just certain parts of the brain—the parts we normally think are associated with mental activity. Is the mind nothing more than certain parts of a properly functioning brain? Does your desire to go swimming actually occur inside your skull, or does your desire cause the neural activity in your skull? Or more generally, in what sense is brain activity responsible for mental activity?

Philosophers typically accept that science could tell us about which neural processes are correlated with which mental processes. For example, it may be that anyone who is depressed has a dysfunctional endocrine system and that anyone who has a dysfunctional endocrine system is depressed. Or, to use philosophers' favorite example, it may be that pain is correlated with C-fiber stimulation: Anytime we feel pain, our C-fibers in our brains are active, and if our C-fibers are placid, then we are not in pain. We actually know that neither of these proposed correlations hold, but they are used here, as they are used in the philosophy of mind literature more generally, to illustrate the type of correlation that some think science will one day reveal. Will science reveal the "neural correlates" of the mind? We do not know. But let us assume that it does. Is the philosophical quest to understand the mind over at that point? Would the discovery of perfect correlations between mental processes and neural processes put philosophers of mind out of business?

Many think it would not, since we would still need to answer why these correlations hold—why, to use our mock example, pain is correlated with C-fiber stimulation. This would still seem to be a mystery, one that calls for an explanation just as much as the correlation between the phases of the moon and the tides calls for an explanation. Others, however, think that the discovery of correlations between mental processes and neural processes would, indeed, solve the mind-body problem, since, as they see it, such correlations would show that mental processes are nothing more than certain neural processes. For these philosophers, there is a simple answer to the question of why pain is correlated with C-fiber stimulation: The correlation holds because pain is just C-fiber stimulation. The uncanny connection between Dr. Jekyll and Mr. Hyde led the London lawyer Utterson to eventually conclude that the misanthropic Hyde was none other than his dear old friend Dr. Jekyll. And a correlation between pain and C-fiber stimulation might lead us to conclude that pain and C-fiber stimulation are one and the same thing as well. If pain is just C-fiber stimulation, if "pain" and "C-fiber stimulation" are just two names for the same thing, there is no more question about why every time people are in pain their C-fibers are firing than there is a question about why every time I shut the door I also close it.

But would the death of the mind-body problem really be as quick as that? I think that it would not, since there does seem to be at least an open question about whether robust correlations between mind and brain would show that certain mental processes are identical to certain neural processes. Though not shrouded in the mystery of a murder—a mystery that begins to unfold only after it appears that Jekyll killed Hyde even though Hyde is found dead by his own hand—the evidence for an identity between pain and C-fiber stimulation still would seem to need some detective work. Although we all understand why shutting the door is also closing the door and how a raisin can be just a dried grape, many of us find it unfathomable that pain is just C-fiber stimulation. How could it be that what I feel in my back when I wake up in the morning is just activity in my brain? A perfect correlation between back pain and certain kinds of brain activity would provide some reason to think that the pain and the neural activity are one and the same thing. But given the difficulty of understanding how they could be one and the same thing, the evidence would seem to be short of being conclusive.

So if correlations between neural and mental processes are revealed, work on the mind-body problem will still continue. If

9

you think the best explanation for such correlations is identity, the philosophical project will involve explaining how we can have an identity between these apparently different sorts of states. If you deny that there is an identity between the two kinds of processes, the philosophical project will involve specifying just what relation holds between the two and what accounts for the correlation.

It seems that even if science discovers correlations between mind and body, there will still be a mind-body problem to solve: specifying why the correlation holds. If the answer to that problem is that there is an identity between the two kinds of processes, then we will still need to explain how there can be such an identity. Might we one day be able to do this? Is the human mind—not merely scientific investigation, but the human mind itself—capable of solving the mind-body problem? Or are we, as the contemporary philosopher Colin McGinn puts it, "cognitively closed" to the solution? Could there be something about the nature of mind and its relationship to body that makes it impossible for the human mind, or perhaps even any sort of mind, be it lesser or greater than ours, to understand the solution to the mind-body problem?

If mind and body exist, there must be a solution to the problem; there must be some way in which the one is related to the other. If there is a solution to the problem, why haven't philosophers figured it out during these thousands of years they have been grinding away at it? McGinn thinks that it is time to give up working on the problem and bask in the satisfaction of at least having figured out that we cannot solve the problem, and he has an interesting theory about why this is so. But many others are more optimistic and see the past as merely a preparation for the solution that is yet to come.

So let us not give up too quickly. Besides, as philosophy is more about working through the processes than arriving at a final product, to give up on the mind-body problem would take away a great opportunity to expand the mind and, as Bertrand Russell put it, to "enlarge our conception of what is possible."

SUGGESTIONS FOR FURTHER READING

Both Thomas Nagel's article "What It Is Like to Be a Bat" and Collin McGinn's article "Can We Solve the Mind-Body Problem?" do an excellent job of illustrating just how difficult the mind-body problem is. Both of these articles can be found in numerous anthologies on philosophy of mind, including the recent anthology by David Chalmers, *Philosophy of Mind: Classical and Contemporary Readings* (Oxford University Press, 1997).

3

A Mad Scientist's Instructions for Creating a Human Being

"In a fit of enthusiastic madness I created a rational creature . . . ."
—MARY SHELLY,
FRANKENSTEIN (1831)

Imagine that you are a mad scientist capable of creating a human being in your underground laboratory. How do you go about your task? Wanting to create something as much like a human being as possible, you consult your anatomy book and get to work. The process takes quite a while, as it involves numerous clandestine trips to the local morgue in search of body parts. And then, of course, the parts all need to be connected in the right way. Eventually torso, limbs, internal organs, face, brain, bodily fluids, and so forth are meticulously inserted, pumped in, and sutured up. After you turn the power switch on, the creature starts walking, breathing, moving, and even talking. All the physical parts are in perfect working order. But is your job done? Have you actually created a human being? Or have you left out something extremely important? The answer depends on whether the mind is an extra ingredient distinct from all the physical parts.

Let us elevate your status a bit. You are now creating human beings in a laboratory well above ground, and not only do you have access to all sorts of body parts, but you also have access to minds. What should you do with these minds? How should they relate to the brain and body? Should they do some work, making things happen in the brain that might not have happened otherwise? As a mad scientist down below ground or a creator up above, one needs to figure out how to put everything together. So let us explore some options that will illustrate positions various philosophers have been drawn to accept, sometimes because of their intrinsic appeal but other times because the opposing views appear to be wrong. In later chapters we will look at arguments for some of these positions in more detail. This chapter, however, is an exercise in what we might call "mind-body combinatorics," as it involves looking at the various ways we can combine mind and body.

The primary divide among philosophers working on the mind-body problem is between dualists, or more generally, nonphysicalists, who think that the mind is an ingredient additional to all the physical ingredients in a person, and physicalists who think that it is not. Let us begin creating human beings in the dualist manner. We will need two sets of raw ingredients: physical body parts, and nonphysical minds or souls. Now, how are we to proceed? One way to combine mind and body can capture a common view about the mind-body relationship, that there is causal commerce between the two. For example, certain kinds of brain damage affect our minds, and our moods affect our brains and bodies. This is the classic dualist position, typically referred to as "Cartesian dualism" or "interactive dualism."

According to interactive dualism, when I think about a sad event, this thought is not something going on in my brain, but is entirely nonphysical. Nonetheless, this thought can cause certain reactions in my body, such as the production of tears in my tear ducts. Similarly, thinking about something funny, which on this view is a purely mental, nonphysical process, may cause my body to fall into a fit of laughter. The interaction goes in the other direction as well. Damage to the brain, for example, causes damage in the mind even though the mind is distinct from the brain. Stepping on a nail causes changes in one's body—a puncture wound, pain signals being sent to the brain, and so on—which in turn cause the feeling of pain in one's mind, a feeling that is something other than anything going on in the brain. If interactive dualism is the correct view about how mind and body are related, a mad scientist, if she wants to create a creature with a mind, needs to have not only a physical body but also a nonphysical mind, and needs to set them up so that they affect one another.

A prominent objection to interactive dualism is that it is unclear how anything nonphysical could interact with anything physical: How could anything as ephemeral as a mind affect something as substantial as a brain? If this difficulty is insurmountable, our mad scientist will need to opt for another arrangement. But which arrangement shall it be? The choice is now between two sets of views: views that reject the interactive part of interactive dualism (that is, reject the idea that mind affects body and body affects mind) and views that reject the dualistic part of dualism (that is, reject the idea that we need two sets of ingredients). If our mad scientist decides to reject only the interactive part of interactive dualism, she will try to create a human being with an immaterial mind, but one that does not causally interact with the body. If she decides to reject only the dualistic part of interactive dualism, she will try to create a human whose mind is merely part of or an aspect of his or her body. The former still counts as a form of dualism, as it involves taking human parts from two different lots: the physical lot and the nonphysical lot. Let us try this approach first and then move on to the latter, which results in purely physical creations.

Let us imagine, then, that after working for months with the physical parts, our mad scientist has created a fully functioning human body, which, if you were to meet this being on the street, would be entirely indistinguishable from a human being produced in the normal biological way. That is, out of purely physical parts, she has created a walking, talking, breathing, smiling, frowning, laughing being. But what about the mind? If the mind is added in a way that does not change the outward appearance of this being and also in a way that the physical body of the being does not affect it, then our mad scientist has just created the type of being we would all be if a view about the relation between mind and brain called "parallelism" were true.

Gottfried Wilhelm Leibniz (1646–1716) advocated such a view, arguing that mind and body exist in "pre-established harmony," running along parallel tracks, neither affecting the other. Leibniz explained his view by comparing body and soul to two clocks running in perfect synchronicity. Once constructed and wound, no extra work need be done in order to ensure that the two clocks remain in harmony. So just as Leibniz's clockmaker would need to perfect the clockwork to create such harmony, our mad scientist would need to perfect the workings of body and mind to ensure that they remain synchronized; for example, when the being willed to raise his or her arm, the body should work so as to raise the arm, or when the being walked by blooming jasmine, the being should experience the scent while next to it and not ten minutes later.

Another variety of parallelism requires constant work for our mad scientist, since it requires not that mind and body be set up so that they run in synchronicity from the outset, but that the scientist constantly step in to assist. Nicolas Malebranche (1638–1715) developed and argued for a worldview along these lines, which he called "occasionalism." According to Malebranche, every time you will to scratch your head, God has to step in to make sure that your arm moves. Leibniz and Malebranche had the same primary motivation for accepting parallelism, and that was their commitment to the nonphysical nature of the mental coupled with their inability to see how there could be causal interaction between something physical, like the body, and something nonphysical like, as they saw it, the mind.

Although philosophers today still debate whether there can be causal interaction between physical bodies and nonphysical minds, the problem of causal interaction is now focused exclusively on one side of the causal relation: How, if the mental is not physical, can it causally affect the body? The line of reasoning is something like this: Every effect that occurs in the physical realm appears to have a physical cause. In particular, it seems that there could be a physical explanation for all our actions. For example, why did you raise your arm? Your brain sent electrical impulses through the nerves that caused your arm muscles to contract in the right way, which caused your arm to go up. And because of this it seems that there is no nonphysical interference in the physical world.

But how do we know that our physical bodies do not sometimes cause nonphysical effects? It seems that just as we have no way of knowing whether there are invisible, impalpable, inaudible fairies visiting our bedside at night, we have no way of knowing whether our physical bodies produce nonphysical minds, if these minds have no effect on the physical world. In other words, it seems that for all we know about the world, physical bodies might have nonphysical effects as long as these nonphysical effects do not in turn have any effect on the physical world.

The view that allows for causal influence from body to mind but not from mind to body is called "epiphenomenalism." On this view the mind is thought to be just a by-product or an epiphenomenon of the brain. If epiphenomenalism is the true view about the relationship between mind and body, then our mad scientist needs to create a physical body and set up the mind so that it can be affected by, but not affect, the body. This is a form of dualism, since it posits a nonphysical mind, but rejects the two-way causal interaction of interactive dualism. The English biologist Thomas Huxley (1825–1895) accepted epiphenomenalism, which, as he described it, holds that mind is to brain as a steam whistle is to a locomotive: The locomotive causes the whistle, but the whistle doesn't help move the locomotive at all. And if our mad scientist is to follow the epiphenomenalist's recipe, she must put mind and body together in a way so that body can affect mind, but not the other way around.

The views we have been examining take it for granted that the physical world exists and that we have knowledge about what the physical world is like. But perhaps our mad scientist questions this. Perhaps she thinks that there are no material entities at all—that everything, in some sense, is mental. Now this view is admittedly rather crazy, but before you dismiss it as one that only a mad scientist could have, consider her reasoning. She knows that she can see her laboratory, but she asks herself, "How do I know that it's not just a figment of my imagination? I seem to see the beakers of boiling fluids, but is it really the beakers I see, or is it only that I'm having an experience of seeing beakers? How can I get beyond the experience of the beakers to the beakers themselves?" The answer, or at least the one she arrives at, is that it seems impossible. The philosophical view that this line of reasoning leads to is called "idealism." As George Berkeley (1685–1753), one of the most famous idealists, put it, "to be is to be perceived" and thus, although the perception of matter exists, there is no such thing as matter in itself; the only things that exist, according to the idealist, are thoughts and experiences.

Epiphenomenalism, parallelism, and interactive dualism all posit that there are two fundamentally different kinds of things in the world: minds and bodies. Idealism, however, holds that everything in the world is mental. Idealism (like physicalism) is a kind of monism claiming that everything is fundamentally the same, whereas dualists say that minds and bodies are fundamentally different. The mad scientist who accepts idealism still needs body parts—legs, lungs, liver, and so on—to make a human being; however, it is just that none of these things, indeed, nothing in the world, would have any material substance.

Now let us look at some views that posit that only physical things exist in the world. These views neither require our mad scientist to work with anything nonphysical nor result in there being anything nonphysical in the world. Typically these views are classified as monisms of the physicalistic variety: They hold that everything is fundamentally physical.

What are you aware of when you observe human beings in the normal course of a day? You see how they move, you hear what they say, you observe the expressions on their faces; that is, you observe their behavior. And unless you are a surgeon or engage in some other practice that uses special equipment to observe the inner workings of human beings, you never see what is going on inside. It seems, then, that the way we know that another person is sad, or happy, or angry, and so forth is by observing behavior. And since we say that someone is "sad" when he or she is behaving in a certain way (for example, head is downcast, the person is unusually quiet and unsmiling, and so forth), it seems that our mad scientist can simplify her life by eliminating the need to add a nonmaterial mind to her creation and merely create a human being that duplicates human behavior.

The philosophical view that there is nothing more to pains, thoughts, desires, and so forth than a disposition to behave in certain ways is called "behaviorism," and it was defended by Gilbert Ryle (1900–1976), who disparaged the idea of the inner workings of the mind as "the ghost in the machine." To be in pain, for Ryle, is not to have an inner feeling, but to be disposed to cringe, move away from what is harming you, and so forth. Now, of course, no one, not even a mad scientist, can create behavior only. If there is laughing behavior, there had very well better be something that is laughing. And so in order to create a being that behaves just like us, something has to be created that is doing the behavior. It is just that whatever it is that is going on inside is irrelevant to what mental state the being is in.

But can it be that all there is to pain is screaming, cringing, and other pain-associated behaviors? At least when stated simply as the view that, for example, pain is nothing but screaming, cringing, and so forth, behaviorism sounds entirely implausible (for can't someone be in pain without showing any of the pain-associated behaviors?), and so it seems that our mad scientist will fail utterly if all she creates is a creature that behaves like us. But if the view propounded by the contemporary philosopher Alva Noë is true, the mad scientist will also fail if she tries to create a human being that shows no behavior at all. More specifically, she will fail if she cannot figure out how to make her creation move around in the world. On his view, called the "enactive mind," how we experience the world is closely linked to how we move around in the world. How we visually perceive a cup, for example, depends on our experience of picking it up by the handle; even the perception of color or the feeling of pain depends on how we are moving about in the world. As Noë puts it, we should not think of perception as an inner process, but rather as something we do.

A number of philosophers, however, think that the internal workings of the body, in particular the brain, are not only relevant to our understanding of the mind, but in fact give us the whole kit-and-caboodle. After all, the brain does seem to be immensely important to our mental landscape. Memories are stored in the brain, many forms of mental illness appear to be caused by malfunctioning neural processes, and our moods are altered when various changes occur in our brains. These philosophers argue for a view of the mind called the "mind-brain identity theory," a theory that came into prominence in the works of Herbert Feigl (1902–1988), J.J.C. Smart (1920–), and U.T. Place (1924–2000). Identity theorists hold not only that our mental landscape is affected by the working of our brains, but also that mental states are one and the same thing as certain neural states. For example, the state of being in pain, for the mind-brain identity theorist, is nothing more than C-fiber stimulation (or whatever neural state is found to be perfectly correlated with reports of pain). Pain exists, claims the identity theorist, and it is activity in the brain. On this view, all our mad scientist needs to do in order to create a being with a mind like ours is to create a being with a brain like ours.

What if, however, our mad scientist fails to find a brain at the mortuary that will be of use to her scheme? If the mind-brain identity theory is true, then she cannot complete her task. But perhaps our mad scientist has come to the realization that it is not the brain itself that matters in creating a mind. What she needs to do, rather, is to create something out of whatever parts she has that will produce all the physical effects that the brain produces and will also react to the same sorts of stimuli.

To proceed in this manner is to adopt a view called "function-alism," which holds, roughly, that mental properties, such as being in pain, thinking about going swimming, and having a visual experience of a sunrise, are those properties of a person that produce certain effects and are themselves responsive to certain effects. For example, to be in pain, for the functionalist, is to have been affected by something painful, such as stepping on a nail, and for this to have caused such effects as the belief that you are in pain, the desire to avoid the nail, cringing, perhaps screaming, pulling the nail out of your foot, and so forth. Now, since the functionalist thinks that it isn't actually the brain that is needed to orchestrate this causal network, she need not look for one. What shall she use instead? If functionalism is true, and she is ingenious, she can create a mind with any number of things. She can find some silicon chips and electrical wires and set about creating a silicon-driven human being.

Is our carbon-based structure essential for our mental activity? Or can a mind be made out of silicon? Dualists think that neither carbon nor silicon nor any other physical substance suffices for a mind. And the last physicalist tactic for our mad scientist to take would agree with the dualists. This view denies that physical activity of the brain or body can account for the mind, not because the mind is something over and above the brain, but rather because there is no mind at all. According to the view aptly called "eliminativism," emotions, feelings, sensations, and beliefs do not really exist.

As contemporary eliminativists such as Paul Churchland and Dan Dennett see it, although we can explain, for example, how genetic information is transmitted in terms of our theory of DNA, and we can explain the behavior of a gas in terms of the laws governing the behavior of gas molecules, we should not expect that we will be able to explain the mental in terms of any other more fundamental theory. And because they are committed to the view that everything in the world is physical, they think that rather than searching for a nonphysical account of mentality, the mind should go the way of witches and phlogiston. Although it was once commonly thought that witches existed, we now simply deny their existence; although it was once thought that when wood burns or metal rusts phlogiston is released, we now deny that phlogiston exists. The mind, according to eliminativists, is more like phlogiston than like the genetic information. The mad scientist who believes in eliminativism (or perhaps we shouldn't say "believes," since according to the eliminativist, beliefs do not exist) doesn't worry a bit about creating minds, since on her view, there are no such things.

So, how would you set about making a human being?

PROJECT SUGGESTIONS

Try drawing or otherwise visually representing the various ways mind is related to body. For one idea of how this might be done, see Richard Taylor's book *Metaphysics* (Prentice-Hall, 1963).

SUGGESTIONS FOR FURTHER READING

Further readings for Descartes's dualism, Ryle's behaviorism, and functionalism are presented at the end of Chapters 6, 9, and 11, respectively. The various other mind-body relations referred to in this chapter are described in detail in the following works:

Leibniz's pre-established harmony is explained in his essay "The Monadology." I recommend going to Nicholas Rescher's user-annotated edition, *G.W. Leibniz's Monadology: An Edition for Students* (Routledge, 1992).

Malebranche's occasionalism is explained in his *Dialogues on Metaphysics and on Religion*, trans. M. Ginsberg (London: Allen & Unwin, 1923).

Thomas Huxley's epiphenomenalism is presented in his 1874 essay "On the Hypothesis That Animals Are Automata, and Its History," excerpted and reprinted in David Chalmers, *Philosophy of Mind: Classical and Contemporary Readings* (Oxford University Press, 2002).

Alva Noë's argument for the "enactive mind," the idea that bodily movement is an essential feature of mental processes, is presented in his book *Action in Perception* (MIT Press, 2005).

The works of the identity theorists J.J.C. Smart and U.T. Place are widely anthologized. Perhaps the most thorough defense of the view can be found in Christopher Hill's *Sensations: A Defense of Type Materialism* (Cambridge University Press, 1991).

In *Three Dialogues between Hylas and Philonous* (Hackett Publishing, 1979), George Berkeley presents a witty dialogue between Hylas, who defends the view that matter and the material world exist, and Philonous, who presents Berkeley's view that matter does not exist and that only perceptions exist.

Paul Churchland argues for eliminativism, that is, that the idea that there are such things as beliefs and desires is mistaken, in his highly readable introductory book *Matter and Consciousness* (MIT Press, 1988).

4

Understanding Dualism of Mind and Body

In any case life is but a procession of shadows.
—VIRGINIA WOLF,
JACOB'S ROOM (1912)

We talk about having a brain and body as we talk about having a hat and blue shoes: They are important accessories, but not who we really are. And when we say "he has lost his mind," it may seem as if the mind is some freefloating entity capable of wandering away from its body. However, just because we speak as if mind and body are distinct does not prove that they are, since there are many things we often speak of that are simply ways of speaking and nothing more. We say "the sun sets," yet the sun doesn't literally lower in the sky. We say, "I'm beside myself," though obviously we are never literally beside ourselves. We say, "I have butterflies in my stomach," but not even the most nervous of individuals has had even one butterfly in the stomach (unless, of course, this poor nervous individual somehow swallowed a butterfly at lunch). So just because we speak of the mind as being distinct from the body does not mean that the mind actually is distinct from the body. The important question is whether we are correct when we speak as if the mind is distinct from the brain.

The question of whether the mind is distinct in a robust sense from the brain is essentially the question of whether dualism is true. But before we ask whether it is true, let us try to better understand the view. What could it mean for the mind to be distinct from the brain? To understand the mind-body problem and to ensure that dualists and physicalists are not talking past one another, we need to make sure that what the dualists are asserting when they make this claim is the same thing that the physicalists are denying.

One idea of what it means for the mind to be distinct from the brain is for there to be no causal commerce between the mind and the brain, that is, for mind to have no effect on the brain. This, however, cannot be what dualists mean when they say that mind and brain are distinct, since dualists often hold that although mind and brain are distinct, they causally affect one another. Or at least "Cartesian dualists" hold this view. According to the Cartesian dualist, the brain can cause certain things to happen in the mind—for example, a brain injury might cause one to lose consciousness, or a chemical imbalance in the brain might cause depression—and the mind can cause certain things to happen in the brain—for example, fear might cause the brain to signal the release of certain hormones.

So, to say that the mind and brain are distinct is not to say that mind and brain have no causal interaction. Distinct things can be causally related: A thrown rock may cause a window to shatter, but the rock is something other than the window and the window something other than the rock. Similarly, for the Cartesian or interactive dualist, although a chemical imbalance may cause depression, the chemical imbalance in the brain is something other than the depression and the depression is something other than the chemical imbalance.

Typically, we think that two things are distinct if they exist in different places: The table I'm sitting at is distinct from the chair, since the table and chair exist in two separate places; tea is distinct from tea cups, since although the former can be inside the latter, the space the tea itself takes up is different from the space the cup takes up. We might call this the principle of distinction: If *a* and *b* exist in different places, then *a* is distinct from *b*. Do we then have an answer to the question of what makes mind and brain distinct? That is, can we rely on the principle of distinction and say that what it means for mind and brain to be distinct is for the mind and the brain to exist in different places?

Answering this is tricky, since unlike tables and chairs or tea and teacups, it is not at all clear where the mind is. Headaches seem to be in the head and a pain in the toe seems to be in the toe, even though aches and pains both seem to be products of the mind. And where are beliefs, desires, emotions, and perceptions of color and sound? Do they exist somewhere in the spatiotemporal world? A thought or mood certainly seems to be extended in time, but in what way could it be extended in space? If we do not know where something is, it becomes difficult to say whether it exists in the same space as anything else. And it is difficult to know where the mind is.

If we do not know where the mind is located, the principle of distinction will not help us in our quest to figure out mind-body dualism. Moreover, some might even question whether the principle is correct, whether things that do not exist in the same space must be distinct. In quantum mechanics there is a phenomenon called "quantum entanglement," whereby two particles can be described only in reference to one another. For example, measuring one particle to determine its spin seems to instantaneously influence the spin of another spatially separated particle. This leads us to wonder whether the two particles really are distinct. The two particles exist in separate locations, but how is the one simultaneously affecting the other unless they actually are not really two particles but somehow one and the same particle?

Although some might take considerations like this to show that one and the same thing can exist simultaneously in two different places, the sense in which these two particles are not distinct might be closer to the sense in which the right half of my desk is not distinct from the left half of my desk: Together they comprise a larger system. Interpreted this way, we do not have a counterexample to the claim that any two spatially distinct objects cannot be one and the same thing.

The principle of distinction, however, may be useful if we interpret dualism as claiming that the mind does not even exist in space (that is, not only does the mind not have any spatial extension, but it is not even in space). The principle of distinction implies that if mind and brain exist in different places, then mind is distinct from brain. Now, if mind does not exist in space at all (and it exists), it must exist in a different place from the brain (or at least, it doesn't exist in the same place as the brain). If so, according to the principle of distinction, it is distinct from the brain. On this interpretation of dualism, then, it is fairly easy to understand what it means to say that the mind is distinct from the body: The mind is distinct from the body because it does not even exist in space while the body certainly does.

23

But should dualists accept this interpretation of dualism? It is not clear that they should. First of all, it is not clear that Descartes himself had this in mind when he claimed that the mind is not extended in space, since something could exist in space though not be extended in space. Trying to figure out what Descartes meant by claiming that the mind is not extended in space is an important question, but let us leave it to the side. Whether or not Descartes maintained that the mind is not in space, it seems that dualists today should not hold this view. Given our current understanding of space-time, everything that is in time is also in space, and since dualists hold that the mind is temporal—that, for example, thinking about summer vacation takes up time (indeed, probably time that should be spent studying instead!)—it seems that, unless dualists are to contradict current science, they ought to hold that the mind is in space as well. So the dualist, it seems, ought to assert that the mind and brain are distinct and both are spatially located.

But now we are back to the question of where the mind is located for the dualist. One idea might be to say that the mind is distinct from the brain yet nonetheless occupies the same, or some of the same, space as the brain. (An alternative to this would be to extend the reach of the mind not just to the brain but also to the entire body.) But can there be distinct things that nonetheless occupy the same place? The principle of distinction holds that if *a* and *b* exist in different places, then *a* is distinct from *b*. This principle, however, is silent about whether two distinct things can exist in the same location. Can they? If so, we will have a way to understand the dualist's claim that mind is distinct from the brain.

Let us try to find some examples of distinct things that occupy the same space. When I climb out of the swimming pool my swimsuit is soaking wet. The water saturating my suit and the suit itself are different things, but they seem to be in the same spatial location. Could it be as easy as that? Swimsuits and water as well sponges and tomato soup or bread and olive oil all seem to be examples of two separate things occupying the same space. So it would seem that two distinct things can be in the same place.

But hold on. These examples are not as clear-cut as they might at first appear. Although there is a sense in which the swimsuit and the water are in the same space—for example, when you reach out to touch the suit, you touch the water as well—the molecules of the fabric do not spatially overlap the molecules of the water soaking the fabric. The H_2O molecules permeate the fabric, but they do not permeate the molecules of the fabric. The molecules of the fabric and the molecules of the water will be located in different places. This, then, is not a genuine example of two distinct things that are nonetheless cohabiting.

But perhaps there are more promising candidates for two distinct things taking up the same space. An example that philosophers are fond of discussing involves the relation between a statue and the material out of which it is made. Is Michelangelo's David the same thing as the chiseled slab of marble? The statue and the chiseled slab exist in the same spatial location. The molecules of David even exist in the same location as the molecules of the chiseled marble. But, arguably, the statue and the chiseled slab are different things, since it seems that David could have been made out of another piece of marble chiseled in the same way. Indeed, the pattern of molecules that eventually realizes David can be found in any slab of marble as long as it is big enough. Could a dualist claim that mind and brain occupy the same location, but are distinct in the way that the statue, David, is distinct from the chiseled piece of marble out of which David is made?

The problem with defining the dualist's distinction between mind and brain along these lines is that it does not seem to make mind and brain distinct enough for the dualist's taste. To be sure, David and the chiseled slab of marble seem distinct inasmuch as the statue David would still exist even if Michelangelo had carved it out of a different slab of marble. If Michelangelo had gone to a different quarry and carved David out of a different slab of marble, we still would have the statue David. This is also true of mountains and molecules—for example, Mt. Fuji would still have been Mt. Fuji even if it were made out of different pebbles—as well as numerous other "distinct" things.

Yet the dualist does not think that the distinction between mind and body is as mundane as the distinction between a mountain and its molecules. The relationship between the statue David and the slab of marble out of which David was carved does not suffice for dualism, because once the slab of marble is chiseled in the appropriate way, we have the statue of David. In other words, after chiseling out the appropriate form in the marble, Michelangelo did not need to do anything else to turn his statue into David. Philosophers sometimes use the word *supervenience* to describe this relation: The statue supervenes on the marble. And it is often thought that if the mind supervenes in this way on the brain, the relation between mind and brain is so close that it precludes the two from being distinct.

Have we made any progress in our thinking about what it means when a dualist says that mind is distinct from brain? Must we go back to saying that two distinct things cannot cohabit the same location?

Not necessarily, since there is still another way to think about what it means to be "distinct." The idea is this: When we have genuinely distinct things, one can exist even if the other does not exist, and vice versa. For example, to say that the stick is distinct from the stone is to say that the stone could have existed without the stick and the stick could have existed without the stone. This is close to what we said about the statue David and the chiseled slab of marble out of which it was made, since just as we can have David without that particular chiseled slab of marble, we can have the stone without the stick. But the difference is that with the stone and the stick, either one can exist without the other, but with David, once we have the chiseled marble, we have David. On the view being proffered, to accept that mind and body are distinct is to accept that even if mind and body always happen to go together, it is possible for the mind to exist without the body and for the body to exist without the mind.

Genuine identities, one might argue, are not like this. If George Elliot is identical to Mary Anne Evans, then anytime George Elliot exists, Mary Anne Evans exists, and vice versa—for George Elliot and Mary Anne Evans are one and the same person, "George Elliot" just being the pen name of Mary Anne Evans. Of course, Mary Anne Evans might have chosen a different pen name, or might have chosen to not use a pen name at all, but still the person whom the name "George Elliot" refers to is the very same person as the person whom the name "Mary Anne Evans" refers to. And the same can be said for the relationship between Mt. Fuji and its molecules, since even though we could have Mt. Fuji with different molecules, once we have that particular configuration of molecules, or at least that particular configuration of molecules in that particular location, we have Mt. Fuji.

So we seem to have arrived at a notion of "distinct" that does some work for the dualist: If *a* and *b* exist apart from one another, then they are distinct. It is a *sufficient condition,* since any two things that can exist apart from one another are distinct. Whether it is a *necessary condition,* that is, whether any two things that are distinct can exist apart from one another, is an open question. Maybe we are composed of both a functioning body and a soul, yet our functioning body and soul are always present and always must be present at the same time. But a sufficient condition is still quite useful, since the dualist's solution to the mind-body problem often involves showing that such a sufficient condition holds. In other words, one common argument for dualism, as we will see, involves showing that mind and body can exist independently of each other.

Dualism, as we will understand it, then, is the view that mind and body are distinct inasmuch as mind can exist without body and body without mind. The mind-body problem, as we will understand it, is the problem of explaining the relationship between mind and body. Dualism is one response to the mind-body problem, or perhaps I should say one "kind" of response, since there are different forms of dualism.

I have dwelt on dualism here, and will do so in the next few chapters, for two reasons. One is that throughout the history of philosophy, dualism has been propounded by numerous philosophers and is still probably the most widely held view about the nature of the mind in the population at large. The second, however, is that much of philosophy of mind is focused on avoiding dualism, because most—though certainly not all—philosophers today reject it. I will provide some of the reasons for this in later chapters, but let me end this chapter by asking you, "What do you think?" Perhaps you accept dualism, or perhaps you do not. Or perhaps you are still not entirely sure what the view is supposed to be, which is a perfectly commendable philosophical attitude. Part of the challenge of philosophy is trying to address questions that are not themselves perfectly understood.

Whatever your views are now, keep this in mind: The fact that a view is widespread alone does not mean that it is correct! As we all know, many popular views have turned out to be false. At the same time, the fact that professional philosophers tend to reject dualism should not in itself make you think that dualism is false. A philosopher may be convinced, or at least fairly certain (rarely are philosophers absolutely certain), that his or her own view is correct and thus might try to persuade you of its truth. But ultimately, when it comes to difficult philosophical questions for which there are no known answers, one must figure things out for oneself. A good way to begin to do this is to look at and evaluate arguments both for and against the view at issue.

SUGGESTIONS FOR FURTHER READING

For further discussion about just what the theory of dualism is supposed to be, I recommend the chapter entitled "The Nature of Rational Beings: Dualism and Physicalism" in Peter Van Inwagen's book *Metaphysics* (Westview Press, 1993).

For a high-level, detailed discussion of such topics as whether two things can be in the same place at the same time and how a statue might be related to the slab of marble, look into the fascinating essays in Michael Rea's anthology *Material Constitution* (Roman & Littlefield, 1997).

5

Motivations for Dualism

I admire machinery as much as any man, and am as thankful
to it as any man can be for what it does for us. But it will
never be a substitute for the face of a man, with his soul in it,
encouraging another man to be brave and true.

—CHARLES DICKENS,
THE WRECK OF THE GOLDEN MARY (1857)

Throughout history, the view that the mind is distinct from the
body, what we call "dualism," has been very influential. For
example, Plato, Descartes, Leibniz, and Kant were all dualists of one
form or another. And today many people are dualists. From what I
gather based on surveying my students, sixty to seventy percent
accept mind-body dualism. Of course, students who take philosophy
may not be representative of the population at large, but I think that,
if anything, they tend to be less favorably disposed to dualism.

What are the reasons for the popularity of dualism? Certainly
some of its popularity is derived from religion, since nearly all the
major religions advocate dualism of body and soul. While religious
beliefs tend to be supported by faith, philosophers typically want
arguments for a view. What then are some arguments for the view
that the mind is distinct from the brain?

The best argument for dualism would be based on scientific
evidence of immaterial minds. If the theory of mind-body dualism
were backed up by scientific evidence, there would be very few

philosophers still arguing over its truth. But what sort of scientific evidence could there be for dualism?

If the soul has weight, then might our bodies weigh less after death? In 1907 a doctor named Duncan MacDougall tried to test this theory by placing dying people on a bed that acted as a scale and recording any changes of weight at the moment of death. (Just in case you are wondering, he claims to have received their prior consent.) What was the result? MacDougall thought that the experiment indicated that the soul has weight and that it leaves the body at death. He reasoned that the change of weight could not be due to evaporation of fluids into the air, since he determined that although this does occur, it occurs slowly and gradually. Moreover, as he pointed out to some of his critics, all fluid excretions that did not evaporate would remain on the scale. He even determined that the difference in weight could not be due to air leaving the lungs at the time of death, since when both he and his assistant tried exhaling a deep breath on the scale, they found that their weight remained constant. MacDougall's experiment, however, has been largely discredited due to its small sample size. There were only six subjects (one suspects he perhaps had trouble securing the consent of more than six), and among these six only in one instance did the individual seem to lose weight at the moment of death (about three-quarters of an ounce).

What would be revealed if MacDougall's experiments were verified? That is, what would be revealed if it really were true that as soon you die, your bodily weight is decreased? Would it be a scientific proof that the mind is really nonphysical, that you really do have a soul with mass? Clearly such news would cause quite a stir. But still more would be needed to convince most of those who reject dualism and the idea that we have souls, since there might be some yet undiscovered physical process that was responsible for a sudden loss of weight at the time of death. At the same time, it is not clear what would be shown if we found no change in weight upon weighing someone immediately before and after death. Although one possible explanation for this would be that the body remained intact (no bodily fluids have rapidly evaporated, for example) and there is nothing more to us than body, another possible explanation would be that the body remained intact and the soul left the body, though, since the soul has no mass, no change in weight was registered. The idea of weighing the body immediately before and immediately after death has not taken us very far, so let us look at others tests and other forms of evidence that might indicate whether the mind is distinct from the body.

Some think that the existence of extrasensory perception shows that the mind is distinct from the brain. In one form of extrasensory perception, telepathy, the mind is thought to be in direct communication with other minds so that one can know what someone else is thinking without any external clues, such as speech, facial expression, behavior, and so on. The idea is that nonphysical minds, since often they are thought to be able to act in ways contrary to the natural order, could perform such a feat but that anything physical could not.

The first thing to say about this argument is that even though all of us have probably occasionally been awed by such things as a long lost friend sending an e-mail just at the moment we are e-mailing that friend or picking up the phone to call someone just as that person is calling us, there is no clear scientific evidence that telepathy and other paranormal phenomena exist. To be sure, such phenomena might nonetheless exist, eluding detection by standard experimental protocols, but even if they were to exist, it is not clear that they would show that the mind is distinct from the brain. Telepathy is odd, to be sure. If it does exist, however, it would seem reasonable to try to figure out how the brain can manage such a remarkable feat. Just as certain animals seem to be able to detect earthquakes based on subtle physical clues that go unrecognized by humans, it may be that those who claim to have telepathy are extremely good at picking up certain social clues that go undetected by the majority of the population.

What if we were to find that telepathy exists between people who are located in distant lands? Then some other sort of explanation would be needed. But even here, the first thing most scientists would want to do would be to try to find out how this could happen given that we are purely physical. Perhaps some people have brains that detect changes in energy of distantly located brains and are able to make judgments about others' minds based on the information reaped in this way. This is admittedly outlandish and almost certainly does not happen, yet the same is so of telepathy: Almost certainly, it does not occur.

But even if telepathy were to occur, it seems that some sort of explanation in terms of neural processes or social interactions (as opposed to spooky mental powers) might be possible. Moreover, even if the mind is distinct from the brain, it is not clear how the existence of telepathy could be explained. In some way, it would seem to be the result of something like pure thought reaching out and interacting with other pure thought. But what exactly this amounts to would require a great deal of explanation. So the mere existence of telepathy or other forms of extrasensory perception does not seem to show that the mind is distinct from the brain.

Of course, clear scientific evidence for the mind being distinct from the brain could arrive in the form of a neuroscientific discovery of a pure mental soul. Imagine the headlines: SOUL DISCOVERED BY MIT NEUROSCIENTISTS DURING MRI SCAN! But while we may be able to imagine this headline, it is very difficult to understand what it could mean. How could a soul be discovered, especially during an MRI scan? Science has discovered outlandish things before, so even discovering souls in human brains is not completely beyond the realm of possibility. Nonetheless, we currently have no idea how such a discovery would be possible.

What does this current lack of evidence for dualism as well as our inability even to see what could count as future evidence imply about the truth of dualism? One thing it shows is that currently there is no scientific reason to accept dualism. However, this does not mean that there is no reason at all to accept dualism. Rather, many hold that there are good philosophical reasons to accept dualism despite the current lack of scientific evidence. Let me then sketch some of these reasons here, and in later chapters, we will examine a few of the more important arguments in detail.

One reason to accept dualism is that unless dualism is true, it is difficult to understand how we have free will. The physical world, as far as we understand it, is entirely law-governed. Some of these laws are what we might think of as strictly deterministic; they say that given one event (for example, the striking of a match), another sort of event must happen (the lighting of a flame). Others are only probabilistic; they say that given one event, another sort of event must happen with such and such probability. However, the life of the mind seems to be neither deterministically nor probabilistically law-governed. You can, it seems, simply decide to raise your arm, for example. The choice to move the arm, it seems, is entirely up to you and not in some sense determined by the laws of nature. Try it, and you'll see: You can decide whenever you want to raise your arm. How could there be a law that tells you when exactly you will make this decision or even tells you how probable it is?

Of course, it may be that after you make your decision to raise your arm, your arm fails to rise. Perhaps at the moment you made your decision someone held it down, or you became paralyzed, or your thought that it would be silly to raise your arm got in the way. But even if the arm does not rise because of a physical handicap or emotional fear, you are still free to *decide* to raise your arm. It is this decision that you, rather than the laws of nature, seems to determine. If this is so, then some mental processes are not law-governed, for the laws of science don't leave anything simply up to us. But the workings of the brain are entirely law-governed. Thus, the existence of free will seems to pose a problem for any view that identifies the mind with certain aspects of the brain, or with any physical system at all.

This line of reasoning is not entirely successful, however, because the question of whether we actually have free will is hotly debated. Although many philosophers agree that it feels as if we have free will, many are skeptical about whether this feeling corresponds to anything in the world that is genuinely free. In other words, although it might feel to you as if you can freely choose to raise your arm, your decision is entirely determined by the laws of nature because your decision is really nothing other than something going on in your brain. And everything going on in your brain is determined by the laws of nature. So free will may be an illusion. And if so, it presents us with no reason to accept dualism. But if it is an illusion, it is one that is almost impossible to give up.

The relation, then, between free will and dualism is this: As we understand it now, neuronal activity follows strict deterministic laws. Yet the mind, if free, would not follow such laws. This fact indicates the mind is fundamentally different from the brain, indeed fundamentally different from material things in general, all of which operate in accordance with deterministic or probabilistic laws of nature. If one accepts free will, then, it seems that the mind is not a material thing. And the view that the mind is not material is the central tenant of dualism. But, again, the "if" is important, for there is no consensus as to the status of free will. (We will return to the topic of free will later in the book. For now, we just flag it as at least a possible problem for physicalism.)

Another reason why you might accept dualism is that you think that it is the only position that can explain how you can have a unified, integrated perspective on the world. Look at the scene before your eyes: You see objects with shapes and colors, objects that you categorize in certain ways, and you see the movements of objects you both hear and smell. All of our senses somehow work together to give us a unified perspective on the world. This is what is referred to as the "unity of consciousness." Yet in the brain, at least as far as we know, there are just billions of neurons firing in intricate and complex patterns. But how can complex working of neurons account for such a unified experience unless there is a physical location in the brain where everything comes together? As far as we know, no such location exists that unifies our experience; no such location exists to create your unified experience of, say, a bell that has a sound and a color, or an icicle that is both cold and hard, or of the room around you with all its sights, sounds, smells, and so forth.

The idea that our thoughts and decisions are free and the idea that our minds provide us with a unified perspective on the world are two different ways of saying that the mind has certain features that nothing else in the physical world has. And if the mind has certain features nothing in the physical world has, it would seem that the mind is not part of the physical world. That is, it would seem that the mind is nonphysical, and thus dualism is true. The mind has other features that also seem not to sit easily in a purely physical world. Thoughts seem to be about things in the world. I can think about the bowl of radishes sitting on my dining room table, and this thought is about the radishes. Yet material things do not seem to be in and of themselves about anything. The radishes themselves, for example, are just radishes and are not about anything else. The table is just a table, and so forth. Neither the radishes nor the table represents or is about other things in the world. But minds seem to have the singular ability to reach out to things in the world and represent them without physically touching them. How is this possible if the mind is something physical, something that is clearly more complex than radishes but not different in kind?

Of course, a book may be about the life of a prince, and a work of art may be about the Spanish Revolution, but it does seem that there is something different between the way in which my thought can be about a bowl of radishes and the way books can be about characters or paintings can be about events. Books and paintings are about things, it seems, only inasmuch as we take them to be about things. For example, in a world where no intelligent creatures existed, if the surf, by a very strange coincidence, washed up driftwood that formed the pattern of the words of the Declaration of Independence, what would this show? It seems that without any intelligent creatures to interpret these pieces of driftwood, the pattern that was washed up would not mean or be about anything. Yet whether my thoughts are about radishes or independence or something else has nothing to do with whether there are other intelligent beings interpreting my thoughts as being about radishes, independence, philosophy, and so forth.

Although thoughts have the property of being about other things in the world—a property philosophers refer to as "intentionality"— sensations, such as the sensation of pain, have the property of feeling a certain way, what some philosophers call "qualia." And just as it is difficult to see how something in the physical world could be about something else, it is difficult to see how something in the physical world could have feelings. I feel pain when poked with a sharp object; chairs and tables do not. When I look at a red sunset, I experience the sunset, or as philosophers like to put it, "there is something it is like" for me to see it. Yet, presumably, there is nothing it is like for my camera to "look" at the same scene. Of course, our brains are much more complex than chairs, tables, and cameras. However, it is not clear how more complexity helps to produce either intentionality or qualia. We can make a camera much more complex and sophisticated, but as long as it is made out of physical parts, it seems that it will have neither qualia nor genuine intentionality. When we think about the feeling of pain or the experience of seeing red or of hearing the violin, we are again led to the view that the mind has certain properties that cannot be had by entirely physical things. And this might make you question the material status of the mind and opt for dualism.

Or perhaps you see a way of responding to these views. Perhaps you see a way to fit intentionality and experience into a physical world. Or perhaps you think, as do many contemporary philosophers, that even though we do not understand how to fit intentionality and experience into a physical world, there are good reasons to think that they must fit nonetheless. But before we look at arguments for physicalism, let's look at some further arguments for dualism, which is what we shall do in the next three chapters.

SUGGESTIONS FOR FURTHER READING

Duncan McDougall's experiments on the weight of the soul are reported in his article "Hypothesis Concerning Soul Substance Together with Experimental Evidence of the Existence of Such

Substance" in the *Journal of the American Society of Psychical Research* (1907).

An attempt at an extended scientific defense of dualism can be found in K. Popper and J. Eccles, *The Self and Its Brain: An Argument for Interactionism* (Routledge & Kegan Paul, 1983).

6

Descartes's Argument for Dualism

"Lord we know what we are, but not what we may be."
—SHAKESPEARE, OPHELIA IN
HAMLET (CIRCA 1600)

Perhaps the most famous argument for dualism of mind and body is that of the French mathematician, philosopher, and physiologist René Descartes (1596–1650). Descartes argued as follows:

> I know that everything which I clearly and distinctly understand is capable of being created by God so as to correspond exactly with my understanding of it. Hence the fact that I can clearly and distinctly understand one thing apart from another is enough to make me certain that the two things are distinct, since they are capable of being separated, at least by God . . . . I have a clear and distinct idea of myself, in so far as I am simply a thinking, unextended thing; and on the other hand, I have a clear and distinct idea of body, in so far as this is simply an extended, nonthinking thing. And accordingly it is certain that I am really distinct from my body and can exist without it. (*Sixth Meditation*)

In this passage, Descartes tells us that if he can understand how the world could be different from how it actually is, then God could have made the world in that way. For example, if he has a clear conception of the Pyrenees Mountains as being a bit taller than they actually are, then God could have created slightly taller Pyrenees Mountains. If he has a clear conception of having woken up three minutes later than he actually did, then God could have a created a world in which Descartes woke up three minutes later.

As Descartes sees it, if you can conceive something very clearly, this shows that whatever it is you are conceiving is possible. Clearly conceiving taller Pyrenees Mountains shows that these mountains could have been taller than they actually are. Descartes's concern, of course, is not with mountains or minutes of sleep, but rather with himself. He wants to know whether it is possible that he could exist without a body. And he thinks that it is possible because he has a clear understanding of how this could be so.

To get a feel for Descartes's method, try to see what it is about yourself that you can imagine being different. For example, can you imagine yourself with different hair color? What about being left-handed rather than right-handed? Or, if you are left-handed, can you imagine being right-handed? Or what about imagining yourself having ears that stick out more than they do now? I would guess that all of this is rather easy to do. And so, according to Descartes, this means that it is possible for you to have different hair color, or to be left-handed, and so forth. That is, you still could be you, but with blond hair, for example, rather than brown. But can you imagine yourself as being radically different? For example, can you imagine yourself as not having any arms at all? I suppose this is not so difficult, as there are individuals who have no arms.

But let us take this line of thought further: Can you imagine being just an unattached head? Or, perhaps even worse, can you imagine just having a headless body, capable of moving and touching things but not seeing, speaking, tasting, or hearing? This, you may be thinking, is certainly impossible: One simply cannot exist without a head. But perhaps we shouldn't reach this conclusion too quickly. Although Descartes does not say that he can *imagine* himself without a head, since imagination, for Descartes, always involves creating a picture in one's mind of something, he does say that he has a clear and distinct idea of himself as a thinking, unextended thing, taking up no space. (It's rather difficult to picture something that does not take up space.) And if he has a clear understanding of this, then, as he sees it, God could have created the world to match this. In other words, God could have created a world in which Descartes has neither head nor body.

Apart from arguing that his mind could exist without a body, he also argues that his body could exist without a mind. His reasoning is parallel: He can perfectly understand his body as a purely extended nonthinking thing, and it is possible that his body could function without his mind. And since both of these are possible, Descartes concludes that he really is something other than his body.

How does Descartes's conclusion that he is distinct from his body follow from his argument about what he understands? Let us look at his starting point: that everything he clearly and distinctly understands is capable of being created by God so that it corresponds exactly with his understanding. How does he know God can do this? If God is omnipotent, God can do anything. But how does Descartes know that God is omnipotent? Moreover, even if God is omnipotent, God still cannot perform the impossible. And how does Descartes know that it is possible to have mind without body and body without mind? Furthermore, how does Descartes know that God exists at all? Although these questions are all well worth thinking about, to explain why Descartes is confident that God exists would require us to go through his proof of the existence of God, which would probably lead us too far afield. Fortunately, one can state his argument without assuming the existence of God. So let's look at how this might be done.

Rather than arguing that mind can exist as a pure thinking thing because God is capable of creating anything that you can clearly understand, we can simply cut to the chase and state that anything that you understand completely can exist just as you understand it. Or in other words, when you really understand how something could be possible, then it is possible. Is this a plausible principle? I understand how humans could have evolved differently, say, to have slightly better vision or longer toes. I understand how I could have missed the bus this morning. And both of these things seem possible. Moreover, try as I may, I cannot understand how there could be a round square. So this I judge to be impossible. Does this show that whatever we can understand is possible?

Much of the answer to this question depends on what is meant by "understanding something" or having a "clear and distinct idea of something." Often we say that a person does not understand something unless what he or she is purportedly understanding is true. For example, we say that the second-century Greek astronomer Ptolemy did not really understand the cosmos, since he believed that the earth stood at its center. If this is how we are to understand *understanding,* then if you understand how something is possible, it is true that it is possible. In this sense, if Descartes understands how his mind could be just a thinking thing without any extension in space, then it is true that his mind could be pure thought without extension in space. And if he can understand how his body could exist without any thought occurring in it, then it is possible for his body to exist without any thought occurring in it.

But there is another sense of *understanding* that doesn't imply that whatever is understood is true. For example, someone tells you about the theory that the first living creatures on earth were brought to earth via a meteor. You might respond by saying that you understand the view but do not believe it. Understanding something here means finding no contradiction in it. This is probably what Descartes means when he says that he understands how his mind could be an unextended thinking thing: Although the idea of a round square is contradictory, he finds no contradiction in the idea that mind is simply a thinking thing without any extension and that body is simply an extended thing without any thought.

Is this a good guide to what is possible? To be sure, sometimes we might think that something is not contradictory, but it actually is. For example, in considering prime numbers, Jill might think that there is no contradiction in the idea that there is a largest prime number, but since as Euclid proved there are infinitely many prime numbers, a largest prime number is impossible. (If there were only finitely many, then you could multiply them together and add one, which would produce a number having a prime factor not on the original list.) But did Jill really understand the idea of there being a largest prime number?

It seems that in relatively simple situations, not finding a contradiction, or an impossibility, in what you are considering is enough to show beyond reasonable doubt that what you are considering is possible. For example, you consider the amount of leftovers on the serving plate and the size of the plastic container into which you are considering placing them. Here, if it seems to you that they will fit, it is reasonable to conclude that they will fit and pour them in. However, when it comes to more abstruse situations, our ability to detect whether there is a contradiction in what we are conceiving is much more volatile. And existing without a body is a rather abstruse situation. It might seem to Descartes that he can, but perhaps he is mistaken.

For the sake of argument, however, let us assume that what seems to be so about the mind, really is so. That is, let us assume that it is possible for the mind to exist without the body. But what does this possibility show? Descartes's conclusion is not just that it is possible that the mind is not a material entity, but that he (or his mind—for Descartes, he and his mind are one and the same) actually is distinct from his body. How does he arrive at this conclusion? How does the possibility of mind and body being distinct show that they really are distinct? It seems as if a bit of magic is needed in order to move from a possibility to an actuality. How does Descartes do it? The principle that contains the magic is Descartes's claim that if it is possible that two things can be separated, then they are really distinct. In other words, if two things are not really distinct, then it is not possible to separate them. Should we accept this?

Think about a true identity, expressed by two different names for the same thing, such as the identity of George Elliot and Mary Anne Evans. Here we have one and the same thing, and not two distinct things. Given this, it is not possible to have George Elliot without Mary Anne Evans or Mary Anne Evans without George Elliot: Wherever George Elliot goes, Mary Anne Evans goes, and wherever Mary Anne Evans goes, George Elliot goes. Of course, Mary Anne Evans didn't adopt the pen name "George Elliot" until she started writing novels. But this doesn't mean that before Mary Anne Evans started writing novels the person referred to by the name "George Elliot" did not exist. The name "George Elliot" may not have existed prior to that time (or if it did, it referred to someone else), but the person the name identifies did exist. And if the name "George Elliot" identifies the very same person as "Mary Anne Evans," it really is impossible to have the one person without the other.

According to Descartes, the relationship between mind and brain is the same: If mind is identical to brain, you can't have mind without brain, and you can't have brain without mind. However, according to Descartes, we can have a mind without a brain and a brain without a mind, so mind and brain are not identical.

Is this magic? Or is it good, sound philosophy? Whether you agree with the principle that allows us to move from the possibility of separation to a real distinction, there are a number of other questions you should ask about Descartes's argument. One is whether a thinking thing, or even thought itself, can take up no space. From what I can tell via introspection, Descartes is correct in saying that thoughts do not fill up space. I am thinking about the beach ball I lost this summer at the beach. The beach ball itself takes up space, but the thought doesn't seem to. And certainly a room full of Nobel Prize winners has never gotten overcrowded because of all the deep thinking going on.

But then again, when I'm thinking, my thoughts proceed in time, and contemporary physics tells us that time also takes up space. So mustn't Descartes be confused in thinking that the mind fails to take up space? This depends in part on whether Descartes thinks that the mind merely fails to take up space or fails to exist in space entirely. Contemporary physics posits point particles, which are thought to exist in space but have no extension. But must we reject the view that mind does not exist in space? The answer to this question depends on whether you think that science, or in this case contemporary physics, should be given the final word about what the world is like. Some philosophers, called "naturalists," think that it should, while others think that it should not. The "non-naturalists" would say that philosophical investigation might be able to tell more about certain things than can science and that, in this case, it reveals that mind is extended in time but not in space.

We should also ask whether Descartes's conception of thought as unextended is really as clear and perspicuous as he seems to think it is. Although Descartes claims to arrive at a clear and distinct idea of thought as unextended, it may be that thought only appears to be unextended. Perhaps if we were to fully understand thought, we would find that it is extended and even that it must be extended. Perhaps when Descartes conceives of thought as unextended, he is like someone who imagines a right-angled triangle in the plane without imagining that when you add together the lengths of the legs squared, you get the length of the hypotenuse squared. Someone who doesn't understand geometry might think that he can imagine this, yet it is impossible for there to be a right triangle that does not have this feature. Could it be similarly that someone who does not understand thought might think that it is unextended even though it necessarily is extended?

Descartes's reply to this line of questioning is that everything about thought is present to his mind. Thought, as he sees it, has no hidden features. Is this correct? Are thoughts, unlike other things in the world, entirely present to us? To be sure, it does seem that we are aware of our thoughts in a special way, and that the way we are aware of our thoughts differs from the way we are aware of external things or other aspects of our bodies, such as the circulatory system. To discover what my circulatory system is doing right now would likely involve a trip to the hospital where I would need to undergo numerous tests. But to find out what I am thinking right now requires only a bit of introspection.

Nonetheless, it is not at all clear that *everything* about thought is present to the person who is thinking. For example, it seems that sometimes when I am not thinking about a problem, the solution to it can just pop into my head. In this situation, it seems that my mind must have been diligently hammering away at the problem without my being aware of it. If this is correct, it seems there are aspects of thought of which we are unaware. But perhaps it is wrong for me to say that the problem solving was occurring in my mind. We could preserve Descartes's view that everything about the mind is present to the subject if we thought that in this situation, the problem solving occurs in the brain rather than the mind even though the solution becomes present to the mind.

My final question for Descartes is: How are we supposed to make sense of an immaterial mind? A mind that takes up no space but nonetheless exists in space would not obviously contradict contemporary physics. It is still difficult to imagine what such a mind is like. Where would it be? When I think about a mind floating freely from its body, I tend to imagine some sort of translucent ghostly entity moving about. However, this is not the picture of mind Descartes relies on, since the ghost that I am thinking about is extended in space while Descartes thinks that the mind is not. No doubt, there is a better way to think about an immaterial mind. But let us leave these musings aside to see, in the next chapter, if we can more easily understand body without mind than mind without body.

SUGGESTIONS FOR FURTHER READING

For the source of the argument discussed in this chapter, see Rene Descartes's *Mediations on First Philosophy,* widely available in a number of translations. The one I used here is by J. Cottingham (Cambridge University Press, 1985).

7

The Zombie Argument
for Dualism

He took off his clothes, and in the darkness thrust his
clenched fists upwards above his head, in a terrible tension
of stretched, upright prayer. In his eyes was only darkness,
and slowly the darkness revolved in his brain, too, till he was
mindless.

—D. H. LAWRENCE,
THE PLUMED SERPENT

Imagine that there are two very different kinds of human beings.
One kind is made out of molecules that comprise various bodily
organs, and musculature and skeletal structures that function
together to create moving, breathing, talking creatures that are also
conscious—that is, creatures that have an inner life of thoughts,
sensations, and emotions. Many think that all humans are creatures
like this.

But now imagine that another kind of human being exists as well.
These humans are similar to the first kind in almost all respects. They
are also made out of molecules, the very same kinds of molecules out
of which we are made. And in them, just as in us, these molecules
comprise various bodily organs, skeletal structures, and so forth, the
very same kinds of organs and structures we have that all work
together to facilitate moving, breathing, and talking. What is

significant about this second kind of human, however, is that they have no inner thoughts or feelings. They will scream "Ouch!" when they are pricked with a pin because their nerves will send a message to their brains, which will send a message to their vocal cords, making them scream "Ouch!" But there is no accompanying feeling of pain. They will say "Yum!" when they eat a perfectly ripe strawberry, but they have no sensation of taste. If you were to look at these humans and the first, more familiar type side by side, you would not be able to detect any differences, for they behave in exactly the same way. However, when it comes to the inner lives of each kind of creature, there is a world of difference. The first kind, our kind, has an inner life. The second kind, however, has none.

Philosophers refer to the latter sort of human beings—the ones with no inner life—as "zombies." These are not the lumbering Hollywood variety with decaying flesh dripping off them as they search menacingly for victims. Rather, philosophers' zombies are supposed to be creatures that are exactly like us in every physical respect but lack consciousness: They scream when tortured and complain about the cold just like we do, but feel nothing at all—no pain, no sensations of cold, no experiences whatsoever. Zombies are just like us, except there is no one home. Are there such creatures roaming the planet? Probably not. But could there be such creatures? Interestingly enough, this is an important philosophical question, since if the answer is "yes," the mind must be distinct from the body.

Why does the mere possibility of zombies show that the mind must be distinct from the body? That is, why does it show that dualism must be correct? The idea is this: If the mind is simply something physical, then just as any molecular duplicate of water would be water, any molecular duplicate of a creature with a mind would result in another creature with a mind. In other words, if physicalism is true, the mind is not entirely distinct from the molecules that compose it. Or, in other words, if physicalism is true, mind is nothing over and above body. Yet if zombies are possible, there can be molecular duplicates of our bodies that do not have minds, for zombies are creatures that are molecular duplicates of us without minds.

This doesn't mean that if zombies are possible, they are actually roaming about on our streets. It only means that there *could* be such creatures. Yet, as we said, if physicalism is true, that is, if the mind is entirely physical, such creatures would not even be possible. If physicalism is true, then just as it is not possible for there to be H_2O in its liquid form without there being water, it is not possible for there to be molecular duplicates of creatures with minds without these duplicates also having minds. So if we think that zombies could exist, we are led to accept dualism, which holds that the mind is something distinct from the body.

How does one go about proving the possibility of zombies? Finding an actual zombie would prove it, but there does not seem to be any; and anyway, we do not need to prove that zombies actually exist. But there is nothing in the world that we could point to and say, "Ah, there we have it, a possible zombie," since everything that exists actually exists. There are no things in the world that are just possible things. Rather, to argue for the possibility of zombies, the dualist needs to argue that even though zombies do not exist, there is nothing contradictory or impossible about the existence of such creatures. One common way to argue for this is with a thought experiment such as the one I presented earlier. I asked you to imagine a molecular duplicate of us without sensations or conscious thought. If you can clearly imagine such a thing, it would seem that there is nothing contradictory about the notion of a zombie. And if there is nothing contradictory about the notion of a zombie, then zombies are possible.

This philosophical method should sound familiar, since we have already come across it in the previous chapter in trying to determine whether mind can exist without body. Recall that there are certain things that we cannot imagine, such as a perfectly square circle. Try as hard as you can, it simply can't be done. And this is not surprising, since the notion of a square circle is contradictory: It is impossible for something to be both a square and a circle. Other things, however, we can imagine. For example, imagine that this book is placed on your desk (or wherever it happens to be) in a slightly different location, perhaps slightly to the right. I take it that you can imagine this quite clearly and easily. And this is not surprising either, for it would seem that it is entirely possible for this book to be slightly to the right. In this way, our imagination is a guide to what is possible.

Of course, not any sort of imaginative endeavor works as a guide to possibility. However, philosophers often—though not invariably— think that as long as we have a good grasp of the building blocks of what we are trying to imagine, then if we succeed in our imaginative endeavor, what we imagine is possible, and if we fail it is impossible. For example, we all have a good grasp of what a circle is and of what a square is, and so the impossibility of imagining a square circle shows that square circles could not exist. Since we all have a good grasp of a book being at a different location, the possibility of imagining the book in a different location is supposed to show that the book could be at that location.

Those who rely on the possibility of zombies to argue for the view that the mind is distinct from the body think that our ability to imagine zombies is similar to our ability to imagine a book in a different location. It is assumed that we all have a good idea of what consciousness is like and what the physical workings of our bodies are like, and so the possibility of imagining the physical workings of our bodies without consciousness is supposed to indicate that such a thing is possible, that is, that zombies could exist.

So, have we proved that the mind is distinct from the body? Although some philosophers are persuaded by this line of reasoning to accept dualism, a number of questions remain. As in the last chapter, one question that may come to mind is whether we really have a clear understanding of the physical workings of bodies. Can we clearly imagine all our physical processes occurring without consciousness? It might seem that we can imagine functioning bodies without con- sciousness, but this might be only because we do not have a clear idea of what we are imagining. That is, imagining zombies might be like looking at a very complicated engine that we do not understand and imagining that it is capable of powering an automobile to drive at 1,000 miles an hour. I might think that I am capable of imagining this, but it could be that I do not fully understand the engine. And if so, I might be imagining something that is not really possible.

Similarly, it might seem that we can imagine creatures that are molecular duplicates of us yet without minds. However, if we do not adequately understand what is involved in a fully functioning physical body, what we imagine might not be possible. Therefore, we need to be careful about what we conclude from what our imagination tells us or seems to tell us. To be sure, we often use our imaginations quite competently to gauge whether something is possible. For example, how do you decide whether your car will fit in a parking space? You try to imagine it. And if you are a proficient driver, you will be correct most of the time. But some may have all the confidence in the world that the space is big enough, and yet end up banging up a fender.

With zombies, could we similarly be imagining something impossible? Or could it be that we think we are imagining something when we are really imagining something else? The answers to these questions are hotly debated. But perhaps you can figure out where you stand on the issue. Try it out: Imagine a zombie. What are you able to imagine? And what does this show about the possibility of such creatures?

SUGGESTIONS FOR FURTHER READING

Zombies come out in full force in David Chalmers's book *The Conscious Mind: In Search of a Fundamental Theory* (Oxford University Press, 1996). For a criticism of the use of the idea of zombies in philosophical argumentation, see Daniel Dennett's paper "The Zombic Hunch: Extinction of an Intuition?" *Royal Institute of Philosophy Millennial Lecture* (1999).

8

The Knowledge Argument
for Dualism

One need not be a chamber to be haunted,
One need not be a house;
The brain has corridors surpassing
Material place.
                              —EMILY DICKENSON (1862)

Pain has a certain feel to it, which is distinct from, say, the feeling
of light touch. The neural mechanisms that underlie pain and
light touch are different as well. But why are they different? Why
can't it be that instead of feeling pain when what we now think of as
the pain centers of our brains are active, we actually feel the sensation
of light touch? That is, why can't those processes in the brain that
produce pain produce another sensation entirely? Or why can't it be
that in me, certain neural processes produce pain while in you those
same neural processes produce the sensation of light touch? Similarly,
assuming that we both have normally functioning visual cortexes,
looking at our brains seems to leave open the possibility that when
you look at freshly sprouted grass, the color looks the way the color of
ripe tomatoes looks to me. Some philosophers think that there is
nothing we can learn about the workings of the brain that could give
us any indication of why a sensation of pain emerges when one
particular area is active rather than some other sensation, or more

49

generally, why the workings of the brain produce any sensory experience at all.

A number of philosophers have taken the idea that from studying the brain we will not know everything there is to know about the mind as a basis for arguing that the mind is not material or physical. Let us examine one such argument against materialism that was proposed by the seventeenth-century German philosopher and mathematician Gottfried Leibniz. Leibniz asked us to do the following:

> Pretend that there is a machine whose structure makes it think, sense, and have perception. Then we can conceive of it enlarged, but keeping to the same proportions, so that we might go inside it as into a mill. Suppose that we do: then if we inspect the interior we shall find there nothing but parts which push one another, and never anything which could explain a perception. Thus, perception must be sought in simple substance, not in what is composite or in machines.

Leibniz, here, is making an analogy between the brain and a machine: The brain is just such a machine that thinks. The brain, as Leibniz sees it, while more complex than a mill, is not significantly different from one, since both are composed of physical parts that push and pull each other about.

The brain is a complex machine, yet as Leibniz's thought experiment is supposed to show, the workings of a machine can never account for our experiences of the world. In other words, minds have certain properties: They are able to perceive things—that is, they can see a flower in bloom, hear middle C on the piano, and so forth—that brains, even combined with the relevant sensory systems such as eyes, ears, and noses (systems that are just other complex machines), cannot perceive.

Is Leibniz correct? What do you think you would find on such a tour of the brain? Today, brain surgeons are not so far from looking at the brain in the way Leibniz imagined going into a thinking machine as into a mill. And in the neurosurgeon's peregrinations around the brain, nothing jumps out as being a perception; certainly, nowhere will one see the flower or hear the note. Of course, many things about the brain cannot be observed merely by looking at it. For example, widespread patterns of neuronal firings might be relevant to perception, yet if you were to wander around the brain, you might miss such patterns. When we imagine ourselves roaming around the brain, we imagine seeing only very minute parts of the brain at a time.

Understanding the mind might require understanding some of the more global features of the brain.

However, this does not really affect Leibniz's point, since I assume he would reply that not only do we not find perceptions when looking around the brain, but we also do not find them when we observe the brain on a more global level. So we must not only imagine knowing how the brain works in fine detail, which is what you might learn on a walking tour, but also imagine knowing how the brain works at a more theoretical level. Indeed, imagine that you had complete knowledge of all the workings of the brain and the sensory systems. What would you know? Would you then understand perception? Would you know what it is to see a flower in bloom or hear middle C?

We can present this question with a different thought experiment, sometimes called the "knowledge argument," from the contemporary Australian philosopher Frank Jackson. Jackson asks us to imagine a brilliant neuroscientist, Mary, who has been imprisoned since birth in an entirely black-and-white environment. She has never seen or experienced colors; she has not dreamt about them or visualized them; she has, we would have to imagine, never bled or even seen her own skin. In this strange environment, she has spent her time learning about color vision and, indeed, has succeeded in learning all the physical facts about color vision. Now, ask yourself: Is there anything Mary does not know about seeing red? Put yourself in her place: Is there anything about seeing red that you would not know?

Dualists think that there is something Mary doesn't know: She does not know what it is like to see red. Imagine Mary leaving her black-and-white environment for the first time. She opens the door and there it is: color! What would it be like for her when she sees color for the first time? Would she just say, "I knew that's what colors would look like all along"? Or would she be surprised? Dualists think that she would be surprised, and what this means, they claim, is that the physical information about color vision did not give her all the information about color vision. Thus, there is something about seeing colors that is left unexplained by the best neuroscience.

But it is not just colors that are not fully explained by neuroscience according to the dualist, for one can imagine Harry learning all about the auditory system while never having heard anything. Harry, it seems, would learn something new upon hearing a trumpet blast for the first time. And we could imagine Gerry who learns everything physical about the olfactory system still learning something new upon smelling fresh-baked bread for the first time. Indeed, there is something about all our perceptions that, according to the dualist, is left out by the best neuroscience: the experience of seeing, hearing, smelling, and so on. If neuroscience cannot explain these aspects of the mind, why think that they are performed by the brain at all?

Perhaps you think there is some sleight of hand here. We have been talking about what Mary (and Harry and Gerry) knows or does not know, but our conclusion concerns the nature of the mind. That is, our conclusion concerns not what it is possible to know, but what the world is like (regardless of whether we know it or not). How is it possible to move from claims about what we know to a conclusion about the nature of the world? What one knows is one thing, while what the world is really like is something else.

This distinction between what we know about the world and what the world is really like is often explained as the distinction between epistemology and metaphysics. Epistemology has to do with what we can know, while metaphysics has to do with what the world is like (whether we know it or not). For example, epistemically, we might be incapable of knowing what color the dinosaurs were, but this doesn't mean that the dinosaurs were no color at all. In regard to Jackson's thought experiment, when we are careful to separate epistemology from metaphysics, it might seem that we can only conclude that there is something we cannot know from studying the brain. What is it that we cannot know? It seems that we cannot know that being in a certain neural state feels like this, where "this" refers to the experience of seeing red, hearing a trumpet, smelling fresh-baked bread, and so forth. But this is entirely an epistemic point, and thus it is still open that, metaphysically, experience is nothing more than some aspect of the brain.

Jackson and others who accept that the argument about Mary shows that the mind is not physical have a response to this line of reasoning. They will point out that Mary is quite special, since she is supposed to know *all* the physical facts. And if this is true, it would seem that if she learns a new fact upon leaving the room, then that fact could not be physical (for she knew all the physical facts in the room). If you know all the facts about the speed of a train and then you learn a new fact about the train, say that it is painted red, then that fact is not a fact about its speed, since you already knew all those facts. Similarly, a fact Mary learns outside her black-and-white room, it is argued, is not a physical fact, since she already knew all the physical facts. Does this argument, then, take us from premises about what we know to a conclusion about the way the world is?

SUGGESTIONS FOR FURTHER READING

Frank Jackson's argument first appeared in "Epiphenomenal Qualia," *Philosophical Quarterly* 32 (1982): 127–136, with a later version of the argument entitled "What Mary Didn't Know," in *The Journal of Philosophy* 83 (1986): 291–295. A recent book, *There Is Something about Mary,* edited by Peter Ludlow, Yujin Nagasawa, and Daniel Stoljar (MIT Press, 2004), presents a number of insightful discussions of this argument.

9

The Problem of Other Minds and the Behaviorist's Solution

By the cigars they smoke, and the composers they love,
ye shall know the texture of men's souls.
—JOHN GALSWORTHY,
INDIAN SUMMER OF A FORSYTE (1918)

Y ou have just finished a scrumptious meal at a dinner party and your host asks if you would like anything else. "No thanks," you reply, "I'm absolutely satiated." Would it make any sense for your host to then respond, "How do you know?" Or imagine your dentist, despite your repeated pronouncements that her drilling is painful, refusing to believe you, claiming that she is a much better judge of when you are in pain than you are.

These situations do not make sense, since we seem to know, and seem to know best, what is going on in our own minds. We may not be infallible in all situations. For example, your best friend may recognize that you are envious, even though you refuse to admit this to yourself, because he was accepted to his first choice for medical school and you were not. But for the most part, the best way to tell how we feel about something seems to be to introspect. We may be able to fool others into thinking that we are not in pain, for example, but we cannot fool ourselves.

Or at least this is the view of a number of philosophers who claim that we can be more certain of the contents of our own minds than we can of anything else in the world. I may be mistaken about whether the temperature outside is high or low (for example, I might think that it is a sweltering day only because I'm feverish), but it seems that I cannot be mistaken about whether I feel hot or cold. I may be mistaken about whether I've been attacked by a mosquito or a spider, but I cannot, it seems, be mistaken about whether the bite itches. As philosophers put it, the contents of the mind are transparent to its bearer. You are aware of what is going on in your own mind.

But now there is a problem. I know what is going on in my own mind. And I know that I have a mind because I can introspect on my experiences, feelings, emotions, and desires. Simple self-reflection appears to tell me how I feel at the moment, what I'm thinking about, and what type of mood I am in. But how do I know what is going on in your mind? Certainly, you can tell me about what you are thinking and how you feel, and I can look at what you are doing and how you are acting. For example, you might tell me that you love the flavor of oolong tea, and I can see that you drink cup after cup of it every time you go to a Chinese restaurant. But how am I to know what the flavor of oolong tea tastes like for you? I know what oolong tea tastes like when I drink it. But how do I know that when you drink it, it creates the same sort of taste in your mouth? Perhaps oolong tea in your mouth tastes the way I experience Earl Grey in my mouth.

Or, to change from taste to vision, how am I to tell that when you see green it doesn't look to you the way red looks to me? More drastic still, how can I even tell that you have an inner mental life at all? You act as if you do, and you might tell me that you do. Our brains might even fire in the same way when we both see green and taste oolong tea. But as I cannot get inside your skin and experience the world from your point of view, it seems that I cannot be certain of anything that goes on in your mind, indeed, of whether you have a mind at all. As far as I can tell, I might be the only sentient creature on the planet, and everyone else may be merely talking, walking, and breathing flesh-and-blood automatons.

This problem—the problem of explaining how we are able to know that other people have inner lives—is called the "problem of other minds." The highly prolific and long-lived philosopher

Bertrand Russell (1872–1970) proposed the following solution to it: You know that other people have minds that are similar to yours because you observe similar behavior and assume an analogous cause of the behavior. For example, when I see one of my students standing up before the class giving a presentation with shaking hands and a cracking voice, fumbling over the words, I can be assured that the student is feeling nervous because I know that when I act in such a manner, it is because I am nervous. Or when a friend presses fingers into temples and furrows the brow, complaining of a headache, I can be assured that my friend is experiencing the unpleasant type of feeling I have when I act in this way. In short, Russell argued, when we observe behavior in others that is similar to our own, we can assume there are similar causes of that behavior.

Something about Russell's solution to the problem of other minds is clearly right: We do make judgments about the inner lives of others based at least in part on how others are behaving. If someone asks for a tall drink of water, we assume that the person is thirsty. But Russell's solution is not entirely satisfactory. Russell is relying on what is called "analogical reasoning," a form of reasoning that starts from the observation of certain similarities among two or more things and concludes that these things are probably similar in certain other respects. But to argue by analogy, you need to make sure the analogy is fitting. For example, it seems reasonable for me to assume that the shellfish I buy at Citarella will be fresh, since every time I have bought shellfish there in the past, they have been fresh, and this time is not significantly different from any of those other times (for example, it is the middle of the week and early in the morning, the same fishmonger is at the counter, and so forth). The situations are analogous in all relevant respects. But when it comes to arguing that other people have minds, we are confronted with two situations that are not analogous in all relevant respects. In particular, given that the problem of other minds is precisely whether other people do have minds, the difference between you and someone else is a significant disanalogy.

The philosopher Gilbert Ryle (1900–1976) saw a different way of solving the problem of other minds. According to Ryle, the dualist who talks about the mind as a thing makes what he called a "category mistake," that is, the dualist makes the mistake of placing the mind in a category in which it doesn't belong. More specifically, the dualist, according to Ryle, takes that mind to be in the same category as tables, chairs, rocks, and trees, but instead of being a material thing, it is a nonmaterial thing. According to Ryle, this is no better than thinking, say, that your college is something distinct from the library, classrooms, cafeteria, faculty, students, and so forth. Imagine that at the end of a campus tour, someone asked, "You've shown me all the buildings, some professors and students, but where is the college?" This would be a mistake, since the college is just these things, and not some distinct entity over and above all these things.

Similarly, according to Ryle, the mind is nothing over and above behavior. Pain, for example, is just the bodily movements you make when you are in pain. The desire for carrots is just the bodily movements you make when you desire carrots. It should be apparent how this view, called "behaviorism," solves the problem of other minds. Pain behavior, such as wincing, saying "that hurts," and so forth, is something that can be directly observed, while the workings of an inner mind cannot.

In thus solving the problem of other minds, behaviorism also seems to some to provide a correct description of our ability to understand language. When you watch children learn language, you find that they use words and perform the right actions to go along with the words even though it seems that they cannot possibility understand the words yet. What they do at first is pure mimicking. Is there some point when some sort of inner understanding emerges? It is hard to see when this would be, or even how such understanding could gradually emerge. Rather, the child's behaviors just become more and more complex without the need for an extra ingredient, the understanding, to be added over and above the behavior. Moreover, if after an extended conversation with you, other individuals behave exactly as if they understood what you were saying (they say the right things in response, have the right facial expressions, and so forth), this would seem to show that they understood what you were saying (though see Chapter 14 for further discussion).

A serious problem, however, with thinking of pain as nothing more than behavior is that you could be in pain, but not show any of the relevant behaviors. This could happen, for example, if you were too embarrassed to show that you were in pain. Moreover, it is possible to wince and say "that hurts" without being in pain at all. Because of this, the simple equation of pain or any other sensory state with certain forms of behavior just can't be right. Behaviorists respond to these criticisms by equating pain not with certain forms of behavior but rather with the *disposition* to behave in certain ways. To be fragile, for example, is to have the disposition to break if dropped on a hard surface. A glass has this disposition even when it is not dropped. Similarly, the behaviorist will say, to be in pain is to have the disposition to wince, say "ouch," and so forth. So even if you are too embarrassed to cry out "ouch" when you fall while ice skating, you would still count as being in pain as long as you had the disposition to behave in the relevant way, that is, as long as you would cry out "ouch" if you weren't embarrassed. Similarly, actors who feel great but act as though they are in pain are, according to behaviorism, still disposed to be smiling, even though while acting they are crying.

Does this line of reasoning provide the behaviorist with a viable theory of the mind? Can we think about pain as being a disposition to behave in certain ways? Well, one problem is that the relevant dispositions have never been spelled out. What exactly are the relevant background conditions under which you would say that you are in pain? What exactly are the relevant mitigating circumstances? It is not at all clear how to answer these questions. Moreover, there are some mental states, such as the belief that seven is a prime number, that do not even have any standard associated behaviors. What does one typically do when one believes that seven is a prime number? The question is rather absurd.

But suppose we could come up with a comprehensive account of "what you would do if" for all the different mental states, and we were able to describe all mitigating circumstances. Would the theory of behaviorism be reasonable then? Since we are so far from being able to do this, it is difficult to say. But one thing is clear: Behaviorism would no longer do the job it set out to accomplish, which was to solve the problem of other minds, because although your outward behavior is entirely manifest to me, your disposition to behave is not.

SUGGESTIONS FOR FURTHER READING

Russell's solution to the problem of other minds can be found in his book *Human Knowledge: Its Scope and Limits* (Routledge, 1992). And Ryle's behaviorist solution to this problem can be found in his book *The Concept of Mind* (Routledge, 2000). Both of these philosophers are consummate stylists and these books are worth reading, if only for the superb quality of the prose.

10

Physicalism or the Three-Pound Mind

Methinks that what they call my shadow here on earth is my true substance. Methinks that in looking at things spiritual, we are too much like oysters observing the sun through the water, and thinking that thick water the thinnest of air.
—HERMAN MELVILLE,
MOBY DICK (1851)

I like nonsense; it wakes up the brain cells.
—DR. SEUSS

In treating people with severe epilepsy, the Canadian neurosurgeon Wilder Penfield (1891–1976) would destroy the area of the brain that he thought was causing the epileptic seizures. To discover what area this was, Penfield would stimulate various parts of the patient's brain with a mild electrical current. Since the brain has no sensory nerves of its own, this was done while the individual was awake. What he found was quite interesting. When certain parts of the brain were stimulated, patients would have very specific memories. For example, each time one group of neurons was stimulated, a patient would remember, say, the smell of her grandmother's attic; each time another group was stimulated, she would recall a certain tune. Does this indicate that memory is just the activity of neurons? Or more generally, does this present a good case for the view that mental processes are physical, a view philosophers call "physicalism"?

Let's look at another example. Certain people suffer from what is called "obsessive-compulsive disorder" (OCD). These individuals are unable to put certain thoughts out of their minds, and they feel compelled to perform certain actions. All of us sometimes wonder whether we left the stove on and feel compelled to go back and check, but the sufferer of OCD will need to do this perhaps a hundred times. Others with OCD might need to wash their hands over and over again. The disease manifests itself in different ways. I actually knew someone with OCD, and the strange way it manifested itself in him was that while driving, he had to constantly stop and check to see if he had run over anyone; driving along one block, he would need to go back and examine the street for dead bodies at least ten or twenty times. For my friend, as well as for others with this disorder, certain drugs seem to eliminate these obsessive thoughts entirely. Since the drugs act on the brain, and the obsession has to do with the mind, does the effectiveness of such drugs indicate that physicalism must be correct?

These are rather tricky questions. It may be that stimulating a certain group of neurons consistently causes a certain perception, yet this alone does not show that the perception and the neuronal activity are one and the same thing. A thrown rock may cause the breaking of a window, and yet the thrown rock and the breaking window are distinct. Similarly, while it may be that changes in the brain brought about by certain drugs affect the mind, this does not show that the changes in the brain and the changes in the mind are one and the same thing. With OCD, obsessive thoughts may be subdued once the person takes the medication, but this doesn't show that the obsessive thought (for example, that the stove must be checked) is just the activity of the brain area affected by the drug. It could be that the neural activity causes the obsessive thoughts but is not one and the same thing as them. So our evidence that neural processes cause mental processes is not alone evidence that certain mental processes are nothing more than certain neural processes.

Nonetheless, you might think that there is still something telling about these cases. And if so, you may be implicitly assuming a principle of reasoning philosophers call Occam's razor, which in one form states that if we have two different explanations for a phenomenon and both explain all the data, the simpler one is more likely to be true. With the OCD example, the data indicate that certain drugs act on the brain to prevent obsessive thoughts and the compulsive actions that result from these thoughts. One explanation is that the drugs are affecting parts of the brain that are those thoughts. Another explanation is that the drugs are affecting parts of the brain that produce those thoughts, but that the thoughts are distinct from the brain. Which explanation is simpler? Well, the second explanation requires us to posit that neural activity can cause changes in a nonphysical mind, while the first explanation merely identifies the thoughts with neural activity. And so the first would seem to be simpler. Similarly, with the epilepsy example, if we say that when Penfield stimulated various brain regions, what happened was that those stimulations affected the mind, a question remains about just how this causation is supposed to have proceeded. To say that the neural activity and the tune playing through your head are one and the same thing eliminates the need for explaining this causal relation, and so would be a simpler explanation.

There is another form of Occam's razor that leads to a similar conclusion. This version of the principle states that when we have two different explanations that both account for all the data, the explanation that posits the fewest entities ought to be preferred, or as it is often expressed aphoristically: Do not multiply entities beyond necessity. In understanding the relation between obsessive thoughts and OCD drugs, we do not need to posit nonphysical mental processes. Since we don't, the principle implies that such processes do not exist.

Are these arguments for physicalism based on Occam's razor convincing? There are a few things to consider before arriving at an answer to this question. For example, is Occam's razor a reasonable principle? Could it be that sometimes the correct theory is not the simpler theory? The principle in the second form says "don't multiply entities beyond necessity," but perhaps there just are more things in the world than need be. (Thoughts along these lines led my dissertation advisor, Bill Wimsatt, to call Occam's razor "Occam's eraser," since, as he saw it, it led us to try to eliminate things that actually exist.) Moreover, even if we do accept Occam's razor, Occam's razor is only a method for choosing between two explanations that explain all the data. But could it be that there are some kinds of data—concerning, for instance, the nature of thoughts—that we cannot account for when we identify thoughts with activity in the brain? Or could it be that nonphysical minds are needed in the world?

If, however, we accept that the obsessive thoughts are distinct from the brain processes, we need to make sense of how to account for causation between physical brains and nonphysical minds. The question of how to account for causation between the brain and mind given dualism was posed to Descartes (who, as we saw in an earlier chapter, argues for dualism based on the idea that he can clearly and distinctly imagine mind without brain and brain without mind) by Princess Elizabeth of Bohemia. Descartes held that mind is "immaterial," meaning that it is pure conscious experience that, as he saw it, takes up no space at all. Moreover, he held that all material things are extended in space. Princess Elizabeth pointed out, however, that it is difficult to see how there could be causal interaction between the mind and the body if this were so. How, for example, could the pain I feel on pressing my finger against a thorn cause me to pull my hand away, if the arm movement is extended in space and the pain is not? How could my desire for a drink of water cause me to go and find some water? Or how could a blow to the head cause a loss of consciousness? All these causal processes are difficult to understand if the mind takes up no space. This question was especially difficult for Descartes to answer, since he thought that for causation to occur, the cause and effect must be in contact with each other, much as a ball is in contact with a racket; and as you can imagine, a ball that takes up space and a racket that does not would not make for a very good game.

Today the problem of understanding how mind and body can causally affect each other does not appear in quite the same form for dualists, and so Princess Elizabeth's criticism of Descartes does not lead inexorably to physicalism. One reason for this is that we no longer think that causation requires contact. Two magnets, for example, can attract each other even if separated in space, and gravity works to pull a soaring baseball back down to the ground. What does causation require, then, if it doesn't require force on contact? This is another big question that has led to an area of philosophical inquiry all its own. But for our purposes here, we can just note that we should not reject dualism simply because it presents us with a difficult picture of causation between mind and body.

Causation, at least as we now understand it, does not seem to require contact. It is also not clear that dualism must be rejected and physicalism accepted because dualists cannot account for how a non-spatial mind can affect a spatial body. The reason for this is that dualists need not be committed to the idea that the mind takes up no space. Certainly dualists hold that the mind is not physical or material, but what exactly does this mean? Must everything that takes up space be physical? Must anything that does not take up space be nonphysical? It is not obvious that dualists must answer these questions in the affirmative.

Another argument that one comes across for physicalism is that dualism is incompatible with the conservation-of-energy law, the law of physics that states that the total energy of any closed system is always conserved. If this were true, this would be bad news for dualists, since the conservation-of-energy law is a bedrock principle in physics, a principle that has achieved both broad theoretical and experimental support. But is dualism inconsistent with the conservation-of-energy law? The reason some think so is that, as they see it, if dualism is correct, then the mind can affect physical objects in such a way as to violate the conservation of energy; that is, it is thought that nonphysical, mental intervention in the physical world would violate the conservation-of-energy law, since nonphysical, mental intervention would create new energy in the physical world.

Dualists, however, have a ready response to this line of reasoning and that is to say that the mental energy acts conservatively; that is, it doesn't create new energy but is just a new form of energy. Thus, the situation that would result if we were to discover mental energy would not be so different from the situation in 1930 when the German physicist Wolfgang Pauli rectified certain apparent violations of the laws of conservation of energy and momentum by positing a new, virtually unobservable form of energy, the neutrino. Along these lines, if we found that mind-body causal interactions violated the conservation laws, this could lead us to posit a new form of energy, mental energy. So it seems that accepting the conservation-of-energy law does not preclude one from being a dualist.

Fortunately for the physicalist, there are other routes to physicalism apart from the conservation of energy. For example, you might reason that while we are far from understanding the details of how the universe evolved, we are fairly certain that the universe began with fundamental physical particles, which by combining in various ways through chance and natural selection resulted in this amazingly complex yet entirely physical world we live in today. Now, where in this story is there room for the nonphysical mental? It would seem that if there are nonphysical minds, then either they or their basic nonphysical parts were there from the start in the big bang or they were inserted somewhere along the line. But, say the physicalists, it seems unlikely that either of these situations occurred. It may be, as is hypothesized by astrophysicists, that hydrogen was created in the big bang, but minds were not. And as for mind being inserted some-where along the line, the physicalists will reject this view, too, arguing perhaps that evidence for this is entirely lacking.

Of course, if minds have evolved out of physical particles, it is also true that at some point, though perhaps a fuzzy one, minds entered the universe. However, this is not the sense of "entering the universe" that the dualist has in mind. The dualistic mind's entrance is rather grander, since it has no precedence. For the dualist, the process of evolution that rearranges physical particles could not account for mind. If mind were constituted entirely of physical particles, it would be physical; but according to the dualist, mind is not physical. And it is the dramatic entrance of mind that the physicalist rejects. So the idea that the mind evolved out of physical particles provides a reason to accept physicalism.

A variation of the argument for physicalism from evolution gets its ammunition from ontogeny rather than phylogeny. For it seems that a human being develops out of the combination of an entirely physical sperm and an entirely physical egg, and that each step along the way from fertilized egg to fully mature adult involves nothing but physical changes. This would seem to imply physicalism, since the alternative explanations for fetal development are unacceptable. (Or they are, at least, according to the physicalists.) What are these alternative explanations? One alternative is the idea that the mind developed from increasingly complex physical components in the sperm and egg, that is, that the mental in a primitive form had to already be in either the sperm or the egg or both. Another alternative is that the mind was inserted at the point of conception. And still another alternative is that it was inserted suddenly (not gradually as would be the case if the mental developed out of physical compo-nents) sometime during fetal development. According to physicalists, however, there is no evidence for any of these possibilities.

But does our scientific evidence really comprise evidence against these possibilities? What we seem to have is the absence of evidence for mentality existing in the sperm or egg, for mentality being inserted suddenly into a fetus, for mentality coming out of the big bang, and so forth. But what does the absence of evidence show? Sometimes the absence of evidence is evidence of an absence. For example, we reject the idea that ghosts exist in part because we have never found anything that could be identified as a ghost. On the other hand, there also seem to be cases where failure to find evidence for something should not be interpreted as evidence that that thing does not exist. For example, the fact that I've never seen bats in my cellar is not good evidence that there are none if I've only been in my cellar during the day.

Dualists might think that the lack of evidence for these possibilities is no different: It may be that we merely have been looking for nonphysical minds in the wrong way, or perhaps we just haven't searched long enough. Moreover, since dualists believe that there are good reasons to take the mind to be nonphysical, the mere lack of evidence for non-physical minds does not incline them to accept physicalism. If you have a good reason to think that something must be true, then despite the lack of evidence for it, you hold onto your belief.

The most widely discussed argument for physicalism, however, is not any of the arguments we have just canvassed. Rather, it is an argument called the "causal argument for physicalism," which pro-ceeds like this. If physicalism is false, the mind is like a ghost in a machine, a ghost who flips various switches in the machine, causing our physical bodies to move. However, we have good reason to believe that all these switches are flipped on or off by other physical parts of the machine. We have good reason, for example, to think that if you move your arm forward to reach for a glass of water, your arm moves because of what is going on in your central nervous system. This is the physical story (the machine). And since it is absurd to think that the switches are doubly flipped by both the machine and the ghost, we should conclude that there is no ghost in the machine—that the mental causes of our bodily movements are them-selves physical parts of the machine.

Is there a ghost in the machine? That is, is there an immaterial mind or soul, working away doing tasks that do not even need to be done? Some dualists think that there is, claiming that there is no reason to reject the idea that our bodily movements are doubly caused, once by the central nervous system and once by the imma-terial mind. Others reject the idea that the machine (that is, the body) is capable of flipping all the switches on its own, so that immaterial mind is needed in order to complete the job. And still others claim that the immaterial mind, although it exists, does no causal work at all, or at least does not cause anything to happen in the physical world.

What then are we to conclude? In this chapter, we have looked at a number of arguments for physicalism, that is, for the view that the mind is a physical part of the body. Earlier we examined some argu-ments against physicalism, for the view that the mind is something other than a physical part of the body. Are the arguments for one view more persuasive than the arguments for the other view?

Or are we in the end left with two conflicting worldviews? One view holds that the world is entirely physical, a view that is motivated by some of the arguments we have just addressed. The other view is that the mental is entirely different from anything physical, a view that is motivated both by a basic intuition that nothing in the physical world could ever account for the existence of minds as well as by the arguments for dualism that we have explored in earlier chapters (such as the argument that a functioning body could exist without a mind, or the argument that someone could learn everything physical about color vision and yet still not know everything there is to know about seeing color). To solve the mind-body problem is to resolve this conflict.

PROJECT SUGGESTIONS

Put yourself in the brain surgeon Wilder Penfield's shoes by applying a virtual brain probe to an exposed brain at "Probe the Brain," online at http://www.pbs.org/wgbh/aso/tryit/brain/.

SUGGESTIONS FOR FURTHER READINGS

Extended arguments for physicalism can be found in David Papineau's *Thinking about Consciousness* (Oxford University Press, 2004), and Andrew Melnyk's *A Physicalist Manifesto: Thoroughly Modern Materialism* (Cambridge University Press).

11

Mind as the Physical Cause of Behavior

You can know the name of a bird in all the languages of the world, but when you're finished, you'll know absolutely nothing whatever about the bird.... So let's look at the bird and see what it's doing—that's what counts.
        —RICHARD FEYNMAN,
    WHAT DO YOU CARE WHAT OTHER PEOPLE THINK? (1998)

When you go about making a go-cart, any number of materials can be used for parts. You might use discarded stroller wheels or grocery-cart wheels; you might make the bottom out of particleboard or plywood; the steering wheel might be a disk or a ring or crossbar handles. Or think about a clock. A clock can be either mechanical or electric, and it can be either analog or digital. A mechanical clock can be made with either a spring or a pendulum to regulate the time, and with either a spring or weights to drive the works. The works can be made so as to need either frequent or infrequent winding.

All this is possible because clocks and go-carts are what they are because of what they do. What makes a clock a clock is that it tells the time; whether it is made with a spring or a pendulum or out of metal or plastic is irrelevant. Indeed, isn't most everything what it is because of what it does, rather than what it is made of? If so, shouldn't mental processes also be what they are because of what they do?

The philosophical position called "functionalism" is the view that mental processes should be understood as those internal processes that do the right job. Pain, for example, is whatever it is inside of you that causes you to move away from the painful stimulus, to say "ouch," to believe that you are in pain, and so forth. Your desire for water, as another example, is whatever it is inside of you that causes you to move your body in the direction of water, think about drinking water, and say, "I'm thirsty." In essence, mind, for the functionalist, is the internal cause of behavior; mind is mind not because of what it is made out of (be this neurons or the material of souls) but because of what it does.

To be more precise, the view that pain is the internal cause of pain behavior is one version of functionalism, and this is the version I shall focus on here. Just so you know, however, a different version of functionalism takes mental states, such as pain, to be the causal network itself. On this other version, pain is not the brain state that causes pain behavior, but is, rather, the state of reacting to certain kinds of inputs, being disposed to say "ouch," and desiring to avoid the painful stimulus.

Functionalism is a close relative of behaviorism. Both views about the mind take an individual's behavior as essential to what is going on in the mind. However, while behaviorists claim that the mind is nothing more than certain types of behavior, functionalists claim that the mind is the cause of certain behaviors. Behaviorists deny the existence of internal mental states, while functionalists accept them. They see internal mental states as the causes of behavior. For example, while behaviorists define the desire for water in terms of water-seeking behavior, functionalists say that it is not the behavior itself that is the desire, but the desire that is the internal state causing the behavior. What state is this? Most functionalists think that it is reasonable to expect that the cause of the relevant behavior will be a certain kind of brain state.

Behaviorism, according to functionalists, though right inasmuch as it ties mental states into behavior, has a number of flaws that functionalism rectifies. One flaw is that according to behaviorism, the mental state of being thirsty is to be defined in terms of behavior, such as saying "I'm thirsty," looking for a water faucet or some other source of water, and so forth; however, a thirsty individual will not look for water unless he or she has some hope of finding it. For example, someone locked up in a prison cell will probably just sit there until the warden brings around the water. And it is unlikely you will say anything about being thirsty unless you think someone might hear you. Functionalism addresses this by adding other relevant mental states to the definition of the mental state at issue. Your feeling of thirst, according to the functionalist, is the cause of certain sorts of behavior, such as trying to find water, given that you have certain other sorts of mental states, such as a *belief* that water may be in the vicinity.

Another flaw with behaviorism is that someone can behave in all the characteristic ways someone who is thirsty would, but not be thirsty. Actors do this sort of thing all the time. But although an actor on stage might act as if he or she is thirsty and may even believe that there is water in the vicinity, such behavior will not have the right kind of cause. Thirst is what it is not only because of what it does, but also because of how it was caused. Thirst is caused by lack of water. Likewise, pain is caused by bodily damage; the feeling of warmth is caused by heat; and so on. Moreover, really being thirsty or being in pain will not only cause you to make certain bodily movements but also will cause you to have certain other mental states. Being thirsty not only causes you to move toward water, but also causes you to *think* about where you might find water. Being in chronic pain might cause depression.

So, although I initially characterized functionalism as the view that mind is the internal cause of behavior, this is just the bare bones of the view. We can now see that functionalism is really the following view:

Functionalism: Mental states are causes of certain kinds of behavior and other mental states, given certain inputs, or causes, and other mental states.

To give a simplified example, the mental state of feeling pain is caused by certain inputs (bodily damage), causes behavior (moving away from the painful stimulus and saying "ouch"), and causes other mental states (the belief that you are injured), given that you already have certain mental states (for example, the desire to avoid bodily damage). Pain, then, for the functionalist, is whatever state is caused by these sorts of inputs, and causes the relevant behavior and other mental states, given certain mental states. In other words, pain is whatever fills the role in an entire causal network. If a neural state such as C-fiber stimulation fills this role, then pain, for the functionalist, is C-fiber stimulation.

Although functionalism is consistent with the view that pain and other mental states are states of the brain, it differs from the classic mind-brain identity theory, since it is also consistent with the view that pains are immaterial states of a nonphysical soul. If there are creatures on other planets, they can count as having minds even if they are made out of some unusual kind of green slime. As long as it performs the right function, the mind can be made out of anything whatsoever. As such, functionalism allows for what philosophers call "multiple realization," which is the ability to be made or "realized" in a variety of ways. A clock is multiply realizable because it can be made in any number of ways as long as it tells the time. Pain, for the functionalist, is multiply realizable because it could be any number of different substances as long as it plays the pain role, that is, as long as it has the right effects, is caused in the right way, and so forth.

The classic mind-brain identity theory, according to which pain is necessarily C-fiber stimulation, does not allow for pain to be anything other than C-fiber stimulation. If there were a creature from another planet who behaved as if it were in pain, yet did not have C-fibers, the classic mind-brain identity theory implies that this creature would not feel pain. No matter how similar its behavior and outward appearance to ours when we are hurt, the creature's lack of C-fibers would imply, according to the classic mind-brain identity theory, that crushing the creature's foot would not cause it to feel pain.

Functionalists think that this shows that the classic mind-brain identity theory cannot be correct. One way of putting this is that functionalists see the classic mind-brain identity theorist as being "chauvinistic" in denying the existence of mental states in creatures that clearly have mental states. Just as John Smith, the CEO at a high-powered accounting firm, is chauvinistic because he refuses to hire women merely because they are women, the proponents of the classic identity theory are chauvinistic because they hold that extraterrestrials cannot feel pain merely because they are extraterrestrials.

Of course, if the only failing of the classic mind-brain identity theory is that it fails to countenance extraterrestrial pain and other mental states, perhaps we could overlook that problem, but functionalists think it is likely that even in humans, pain may be realized in a variety of ways. It will still, of course, be brain states that are doing the work, but functionalists think that it is likely that, to take a made-up example, pain might occur in you when C-fibers are stimulated, but the very same kind of pain might occur in me when A-fibers are stimulated. Functionalism would allow for both of these neural processes to count as pain, while the classic mind-brain identity theory, as it identifies pain with a type of neural activity, would not.

One aspect of functionalism that can be confusing is that it is both opposed to the mind-brain identity theory and also a version of the mind-brain identity theory. But this is not actually paradoxical because the type of mind-brain identity theory that functionalism is opposed to is not the same as the type of mind-brain identity theory of which it is a version. The type of mind-brain identity theory that it is opposed to is what I have been calling the "classic mind-brain identity theory," which holds that mental properties, such as being in pain, are *necessarily* identical to certain neural properties, such as being in a neural state of C-fiber stimulation. To say that the identity between pain and C-fiber stimulation is necessary is to say that whenever there is pain, there is C-fiber stimulation, and vice versa. However, functionalists think that there is a contingent identity between pain and C-fiber stimulation (or whatever state turns out to be the causal nexus for pain).

Another confusing aspect of functionalism is that it defines mental states in terms of a causal network that involves other mental states, and so it might seem that those mental states are left unexplained. But this is not so. Functionalism aims to be a complete theory of the mind. Just as pain is defined, in part, in terms being something that causes the desire to avoid the painful stimulus, this desire will be defined in terms of its place in a causal network as well, until what emerges is an entire network of interdefined mental states.

Functionalism, then, seems to have a number of advantages over other theories of the mind. As functionalists see it, functionalism takes what is correct about dualism, which is the idea that mind is internal and private, but does so without the need for a nonmaterial soul. Functionalists also take what they see as correct about behaviorism, which is the idea that mind is closely connected to behavior, but since the relevant causal network of any mental state includes more than behavior, this does not lead to the implausible view that someone who is acting as if he is in pain really is in pain. Finally, functionalists take what they see as correct about the mind-brain identity theory, which is the idea that mental states are certain neural states, yet allow for creatures without brains to have mental states as well. For the functionalist, the identity between mental states and neural states is just contingent—pain, for example, happens to be C-fiber stimulation, but other sorts of neural or even non-neural processes could be pain as well.

With all these advantages, why isn't everyone a functionalist? The simple answer is that although functionalism does not fall prey to many of the objections that seem to thwart other theories of the mind, some think it is prey to a rather devastating objection itself: that it fails to account for experience. The functionalist picture of the mind is: That which is the cause of certain behavior and other mental states is caused in a variety of ways. But why should this give rise to the experience of, say, tasting wasabi? Whether this sort of objection can be countered is very much a live question in philosophy of mind, and it is one I leave for you to ponder.

SUGGESTIONS FOR FURTHER READING

The version of functionalism I am presenting here is explained and defended in D. M. Armstrong's *A Materialist Theory of the Mind* (Routledge and Kegan Paul, 1968), as well as in works by David Lewis, such as the enjoyable and widely anthologized paper "Mad Pain, Martian Pain."

12

Thinking about Thought

All the colors had returned to their original brightness, and as they raced along the road Milo continued to think of all sorts of things; of the many detours and wrong turns that were so easy to take, of how fine it was to be moving along, and, most of all, how much could be accomplished with just a little thought.

—NORTON JUSTER,
THE PHANTOM TOLLBOOTH (1961)

It is our ability to think that is our greatest strength. Compared to other animals, we fare poorly in many ways. Certainly there are animals that have more physical strength and agility. And there are animals that have keener senses. Bloodhounds, for example, have a much better sense of smell than we do, and eagles have a much better sense of sight. But we stand out in our ability to construct complex thoughts. Perhaps a monkey can think, "I want a banana," and perhaps even, "I'll have that banana when it's ripe." However, the thought, "if I break this tree branch and tie it to the other one on the ground, then I could lean it over the moat and thereby get across to the zookeeper's office and get the key out of the zookeeper's pocket to the room where the bananas are stored" is evidently beyond a monkey's ability. But what is thought? What is this thing that counts as the crowning achievement of our species?

Thought seems to be something that can either go on without our directing it, as when one's mind is wandering, or can be directed, as when we need to figure out a problem. It also seems to be something that can be either conscious or unconscious. When you are trying to figure something out—say, how to begin writing an essay— sometimes you will be consciously aware of the thoughts that go through your mind. For example, you might consciously decide to start with a leading question, and then consciously run through and evaluate some of the possibilities. But perhaps you have also had the experience of taking your mind off the topic for a while and then having the solution just come to you. For example, after hours of struggling to find the right way to start an essay, you might have decided to take a break and go swimming, and then during the swim, even though it didn't seem to you that you were thinking about your essay, an opening paragraph just came to mind. How were you able to do this? It seems that a reasonable explanation is that while you were swimming, your mind was unconsciously thinking things out.

So thoughts, as well as beliefs, desires, hopes, and fears, can be conscious or unconscious. But what makes something a thought? This is a difficult question, and in answering it, one hardly knows where to begin. So let us be a bit more humble and start with a smaller task—that of understanding one aspect of thought: how thoughts can be about things in the world. Right now, for example, I am thinking about thought, and if thought is something that exists in the world, that means I am thinking about something in the world. Thoughts can be about imaginary things such as unicorns or monsters. Or they may be about theories—either spurious ones, such as the way in which the orientation of the stars when we were born affects our personalities, or serious ones, such as the theory of relativity. In any case, thought is always about something or other. Think about a rose in full bloom. Your thought is about a rose; it somehow points at, or represents, a rose. And what goes for thought goes for belief, desire, fear, hope, and imagination as well. These mental states all seem to be about things: If I believe that the sun is out, my belief is about the sun; if I desire a cup of tea, my desire is about a cup of tea. Philosophers call this feature of certain mental states (that is, their ability to point at things in the world) "intentionality."

The word *intentionality* can be confusing, since it seems as if it should have something to do with being intentional, in the sense of being deliberate or having an intention to do something. But intentionality is quite different from the notion of deliberateness. You can have a nagging thought come to your mind, and this thought can exhibit intentionality (for example, it might be about the faux pas you made the other day with a friend), yet you are not intentionally (that is, deliberately) trying to think about this. And typically you do not deliberately believe what you believe; you just believe it. For example, I do not have to try to believe that Chicago is cold during the winter; I just believe it. It is not even clear that the idea of a deliberate belief makes sense, since it seems that although you can deliberately decide to acquire information about, say, the court of Louis XIV, whether you believe the information is in a sense not under your control.

Now, the philosopher William James denied this, as the title of his book, *The Will to Believe*, illustrates. He thought that if the reward was great enough, you could will yourself to believe in God. But even if someone can simply choose to believe in something, the notion of *intentional* we are concerned with is not the same as *deliberate*. Beliefs always exhibit intentionality in the sense of about-ness, but they rarely, at best, are intentional in the sense of deliberate.

The mind is rife with intentionality, and philosophers have thought that understanding intentionality is a crucial step in understanding the mind. This was especially so for Franz Brentano (1838–1917) who claimed that all mental processes are intentional. That is, Brentano thought that everything that goes on in the mind is about something. As I said earlier, beliefs and thoughts always exhibit intentionality. When I am thinking, I am always thinking about something; when I have a belief, it is always a belief about something.

But does everything that goes in the mind exhibit intentionality? The answer, of course, depends on what counts as mind. If one limits what counts as mind to processes that are intentional, then Brentano is correct. But is it correct to limit what counts as mental in this way? Aren't there other processes that would be rightly called "mental" yet are not about anything at all? For example, have you ever experienced free-floating anxiety, where you are anxious, but not anxious about anything in particular? If you have, you know what an unpleasant sensation it is: worry, without being worried about anything, apprehensiveness without being apprehensive about anything. Since anxiety intuitively counts as a mental process, free-floating anxiety seems to show that Brentano is wrong and that some mental processes are not directed at anything at all—at least, if free-floating anxiety actually exists.

Despite appearances, however, it is possible there is no such thing as entirely free-floating anxiety. It might be that when you experience free-floating anxiety, you are anxious about something, yet you are not consciously aware of what it is. Say, for example, that you are planning to go to Mexico with a friend during spring break. While you are packing, you feel a sense of foreboding and unease, which seems to you entirely undirected. But when your friend mentions that you seem to be very concerned about your sister who just got divorced, you realize that your anxiety has to do with leaving the country when your sister might need you for emotional support. So, it may be that anxiety is always directed at something but that sometimes we are not consciously aware of what we are anxious about. Moreover, sometimes what we count as cases of free-floating anxiety may just be cases of anxiety over rather abstract things such as "failure," or "loss," or "disaster." Such anxiety, however, would still be directed, even if what it is directed at is rather intangible.

What about pains, pleasures, and other sensations? Are they intentional? Is pain about anything? There is a sense in which my consciousness of my pain is about my pain. But is the pain itself about anything? Does it represent anything? I feel pain and my pain might be in my knee, but my pain itself is not about my knee. Some philosophers think that in a sense it is: that knee pain represents pain in the knee and, more generally, that pain represents bodily damage. Of course, not all pain arises because of bodily damage. For example, stretching our hamstring muscles after exercise is good for the muscles despite the pain it can cause, or so we are told. And weight training can certainly be painful, but it seems to make us stronger rather than damage us. But, you might say, stretching and weight training are kinds of damage; perhaps weight training causes damage, but just a special kind of damage that makes you stronger.

But what about the pain I feel in my knee that arises merely because I'm thinking so much about knee pain? Such psychosomatic pains are real pains, but are they caused by bodily damage? A pain, however, does not need to be caused by bodily damage to represent bodily damage. That is, just as a thought that bananas are purple represents bananas as purple, even though they are not, my psychosomatic knee pain could represent bodily damage even if there is none.

Whether or not pain has intentionality—and whether or not its entire nature is exhausted by its intentionality, as some philosophers think—many mental states do seem to have it, and it does not seem to occur outside of our minds. Nonmental objects typically are not about other things. My cup of tea, for example, is merely a cup of tea; it isn't about anything in the sense that my belief that there is a teacup on my desk is about the teacup on the desk. A tree is just a tree and a rose is just a rose; neither is about, or directed at, things in the world. Yet somehow our minds can be directed at the world.

But if only the mind can somehow reach out into the world and represent things in the world, and the mind is just a physical system, how does intentionality arise in the mind? How could neurons, which are as physical as teacups and trees, be directed or represent other things? How do we get our belief to be about hot tea if the little bits of matter that constitute this belief do not seem to be about anything? The problem is that if physicalism is true, the mind is made up of neurons, yet neurons do not seem to be about anything. Like teacups, trees, and roses, neurons just are. And if neurons themselves are not about things in the world, it does not seem that complex arrangements of neurons can accomplish the task of being about things in the world either.

Hold on, you may be thinking, plenty of nonmental things represent other things: books, movies, and pictures all represent other things in the world. True enough, but are books, movies, and pictures in and of themselves about things in the world or are they only about things in the world inasmuch as we take them to be about things in the world? Imagine a world with no human beings in it. In this world, some driftwood happens to wash up on the shore and the pieces end up arranged so that they look just like our word *AX*. Do these pieces of driftwood just sitting there on the beach with no one to observe them have any meaning? Of course, as we think about that world, we naturally give a meaning to the strewn wood. Yet we are supposed to imagine the pieces there without anyone to interpret them at all. It would seem that in a world with no observers to interpret the pieces of wood as meaning something, the pieces of driftwood would be just that: pieces of wood washed up on the shore.

Some think that although the driftwood pieces and minds represent in different ways, this difference does not amount to a difference in kind, but merely a difference in degree. And the difference is that when our minds represent reality, our thoughts form an unbelievably complex structure. My belief that Sacramento is the capital of California is connected to ideas about the relationship between states and capitals, to the location of Sacramento in California, to the representation of California and Sacramento on a map, to my fourth-grade field trip to Sacramento during which a girl fainted in the capitol building with a resounding crash of her head on the marble floor, and so forth. Books, movies, and pictures do not come close to presenting the vast number of ways in which our ideas are related.

But is complicating the structure of physical objects enough to give us representation? Can mere complexity bestow intentionality upon something that does not already have it? Take a gigantic pile of chairs and arrange them in a highly complicated pattern; what you have is still merely a complicated pattern of chairs. We might interpret the chairs as representing the mathematical equation that describes the pattern. But the pattern of chairs in and of itself does not seem to be about anything.

Perhaps it is not any sort of complexity that is required for intentionality. Perhaps what is needed is a causal relation between what is doing the representing and the object represented. For example, it is natural to think that the rings on the trunk of a tree represent growing seasons; the more rings a tree has, the more growing seasons it has had. Is there a natural causal relation between beliefs, thoughts, desires, and hopes and things in the world that would make those mental processes represent things in the world? How would such a picture of intentionality account for misrepresentation? Tree rings, at least typically, do not represent a growing season as long when it was actually short, but we make mistakes frequently. Moreover, how would such a picture account for the ability our minds have to represent imaginary things? Those who defend this view of how the mind represents the world need to address these questions.

Does intentionality really even exist? A different response to the problem of how to account for intentionality is to deny that it is a real feature of the world. Perhaps human thought is only intentional inasmuch as others take it to be intentional. Perhaps the thoughts of a lone human being who existed in a world without anyone with whom to interact would not be intentional. These sorts of questions are at the heart of many of the debates about what is called "artificial intelligence" (a topic we will pursue in the next chapter), for if we are to create thinking computers, it would seem that their thoughts would have to have intentionality in and of themselves. Either that, or the thoughts of human beings are not intentional in this way either.

Intentionality might seem especially recalcitrant to an explanation when we take into account that thoughts, beliefs, and so forth can be about things that do not exist. I can, as the philosopher Elizabeth Anscombe suggested, have a thought about a man—just a man in general, not any particular man. But while I can think about a man who is no man in particular, there cannot be any men in the world that are not particular men; every single man that exists is a particular man. So, when I think about a man, but not any particular man, what am I thinking about? What does my thought represent?

This problem appears even more forcefully when we consider our thoughts about things such as fairies, leprechauns, and Santa Claus. We can believe that Santa Claus does not exist. But what is such a belief about? One response might be to say that it is about the idea of Santa Claus. Perhaps, for example, all that I mean when I say that Santa Claus has a white beard is that I believe that the idea of Santa Claus represents him as having a white beard. But this is not an adequate response, and we can see this when we consider the following example. Imagine two children arguing about whether Santa Claus exists. "I know that Santa Claus exists," says one. The other responds, "You're wrong; Santa Claus does not exist." What are these children arguing about? Whatever they are arguing about, it seems that they are not arguing over whether the idea of Santa Claus exists. That is something they both accept. Or consider debates over the existence of parapsychology. If Jan believes that parapsychology does not exist, Jan's belief is not about the idea of parapsychology, since she accepts that the idea exists. But beliefs about such things as fairies and Santa Claus, as well as thoughts about a man who is not any particular man, seem nonetheless to be about things—that is, they seem to be intentional. But if they are not about the ideas of these things, what then are they about?

One answer is that they are about things that do not exist. But the idea of things that do not exist is a rather strange one. What makes a thing still a thing, if it does not exist? If it does not exist, where is it? If the answer is "nowhere," then it would seem to not be a thing at all, since isn't it the case that every thing is somewhere or other? Moreover, if my thought is about something that does not exist, it would seem, on a natural way of understanding this phrase, that my thought is not about anything at all. But how could my thoughts, for example, that leprechauns have green skin and that Santa Claus has a white beard be about nothing? If they are about nothing, are they then thoughts about the same thing, that is, nothing? Surely they cannot be about the same thing, since one is about leprechauns and one is about Santa Claus. What, then, are these thoughts about?

We have been thinking about thought, which is a process that is definitely intentional. But what exactly intentionality is, and how it can do the remarkable things that it seems to do, is still a mystery—a mystery well worth thinking about.

SUGGESTIONS FOR FURTHER READING

Franz Brentano argues for the view that all mental phenomena exhibit intentionality in his magnum opus *Psychology from an Empirical Standpoint*. For further discussion of this view and the problem of how our thoughts can be about things that do not actually exist, such as unicorns, I recommend Stephen Stich and Fritz Warfield's anthology *Mental Representation* (Blackwell, 1994).

13

Can Computers Think?

Program: A set of instructions, given to the computer, describing the sequence of steps the computer performs in order to accomplish a specific task. The task must be specific, such as balancing your checkbook or editing your text. A general task, such as working for world peace, is something we can all do, but not something we can currently write programs to do.

—FROM UNIX USER'S MANUAL,
SUPPLEMENTARY DOCUMENTS

ME: Hello.

ALICE: Hi there!

ME: What's your name?

ALICE: My name is Alice.

ME: May I ask you something?

ALICE: Go ahead. Ask me anything.

ME: What is the meaning of life?

ALICE: Actually, it's twenty-three, not forty-two.

ME: So you've read *The Hitchhiker's Guide to the Universe?*

ALICE: Interesting deduction. I've scanned it.

The above is an excerpt from a conversation I had online. There would seem to be nothing too remarkable about it; however, the individual with whom I was chatting was not a human being. Rather, the responses were those of A.L.I.C.E. (Artificial Linguistic Internet Computer Entity), who, if you ask her to tell you a bit about herself, will tell you that she is an artificial linguistic entity. (Though if you ask her, "who are you?" she'll respond by saying that she often asks herself that question.) A.L.I.C.E., who, as you can tell, is quite personable and often witty, is the outcome of what some call "artificial intelligence," or AI.

But should I really be talking about A.L.I.C.E. in this way? Is it right to talk about *her* rather than *it?* Can a computer program really be personable and witty? More generally, can a computer really think? Sometimes we say that even as simple a computer as a bank machine is thinking while we wait for it to spit out the cash; or after we type a command into our computer and watch while it processes the command, we might feel that we are watching it think. But isn't this just speaking metaphorically? Computers—and especially bank machines—do not think. They are just thoughtless human-programmed machines that do whatever we tell them to. Or are they?

Alan Turing, the British mathematician who cracked the German "Enigma code" during World War II, was interested in the question of whether computers can think. He proposed what some take to be a definitive answer to this question. His answer was that a computer's responses count as thinking if, upon reading the responses, you would not be able to tell whether they were made by a computer or a human being. So, for example, if I had given you a sufficiently long transcription of my conversation with A.L.I.C.E. and you had thought that I was talking with a human, then, according to Turing, A.L.I.C.E's responses would have been the result of thought. This test for thought has come to be known, for obvious reasons, as the "Turing test."

Is the Turing test a good test for thought? One thing it has in its favor is that it is fairly straightforward. Just have a group of judges type out whatever questions they would like answered and submit them to both a group of computers and a group of people. If the judges, who cannot see either the computers or the people, are unable to distinguish the people from the computers, then the computers have passed the Turing test, which means, according to Turing, they can think.

But does merely passing such a test really show that a computer can think? Certainly, if a computer fools us into thinking that it is a human being, the computer makes us believe that it thinks. That is, we will believe that the computers who pass the Turing test are thinking, since a computer passes the Turing test by making an interrogator believe that the computer is thinking. The question is, however, does passing the test show that it really thinks?

Perhaps before addressing this question we should look a little more closely at the test. Although the Turing test is a relatively straightforward test, there are a number of questions we should ask about it. For example, it would be good to know how much time the judges have to ask questions, since a short interrogation would seem to be insufficient. I've certainly been fooled for a brief time even by telephone answering machines, and I have always felt grateful if no one was around to hear me say "hello" back. But I don't know anyone who would say that answering machines think. Perhaps the dialogue with A.L.I.C.E. at the beginning of this chapter fooled you briefly. However, had I transcribed the rest of my conversation with her, you would have found many nonsequiturs that would have revealed that A.L.I.C.E. is not a real human being. For example, after quite a long conversation, I told her, "My plans have changed," to which she responded, "Where did you get your plans have changed?"

For how long, then, does the computer need to trick the interrogator? If we put no limit on the time allotted for questioning, we may in some cases never arrive at an answer. In these cases, all we would be able to say is that so far the test taker is passing the test. (Of course, a negative verdict could come rather quickly.) On the other hand, too short a time, as the opening conversation with A.L.I.C.E. illustrates, is no good either. So what is the right amount of time? An hour? A day? A month? A year?

Another question you might have about the test is whether the type of questions the interrogator is allowed to ask should be restricted in some way. Currently no computer programs are perfect, and someone with some knowledge of the program might know the kind of questions that will trip up the computer. With A.L.I.C.E. we found that she didn't do nearly as well with statements as she did with questions. Also, certain question forms confused her (if *confused* is the right word). For example, if one were to ask, "Did you ever think you might be wasting your time?" inadequate answers might be given, not just because she could not understand certain types of sentence constructions, but also because she might not have been given enough information to adequately answer questions on some topics that any adult human can understand. For example, if she were asked, "Does a tree grow in the ground?" she would readily respond, "If it does, I never heard about it before." This sort of response would quickly tip off any judges, and A.L.I.C.E. would lose the game. So it seems that to even get the game going, we need to give A.L.I.C.E. a bit of a head start by restricting the types of questions the interrogators are allowed to ask. But perhaps this head start invalidates the test.

Yearly, since 1991, there have been enactments of the Turing test, and when the amount of time and the topics have been limited, various astute judges have sometimes been fooled into thinking that the responses of a computer were the responses of humans. Nonetheless, computers such as A.L.I.C.E. cannot reasonably respond to any type of question that may cross your mind. To be sure, another human cannot correctly answer any type of question that may cross your mind. If you ask me who the tenth president of the United States was, I would have to say, "I don't know offhand, but I'll look it up." This doesn't provide the correct answer to the question; however, it is a reasonable answer—that is, it is not nonsense. With A.L.I.C.E., however, we get too much nonsense. But is this relevant? Does the distinction between a machine that thinks and one that does not simply turn on the fact that the one that thinks can reasonably respond to any sort of question while the one that does not will respond too frequently with a nonsequitur? Or might the problem run deeper: Could it be that programmed silicon is just not the right sort of thing to underlie thoughts?

This question of whether or not programmed silicon is the right medium to underlie thought has two aspects. One is the idea that being programmed eliminates the possibility of thought. The other is that silicon-based things are not capable of thought; only carbon-based, flesh-and-blood things, like us, are. Let's consider the first issue. What is it about being programmed that might be incompatible with thought? For in a sense aren't we programmed from birth by our parents, teachers, leaders, and so forth?

Perhaps prior to asking whether being programmed is incompatible with thought, we need to ask, "What is it to be programmed?" Sometimes people think that if a computer is programmed, then it has all of its responses written into it in advance by someone (or something) else. In order to answer the question "How are you?" such a computer would search through a list of questions, find the one that matches "How are you?" and then give as output the answer that is correlated with it, which presumably will be something like, "Fine, and you?" If this were all there was to being programmed, being programmed might seem to exclude thought. Of course, at certain times our answers have the feel of merely being retrieved from a list. For example, for me, the question "how are you?" does seem to merely cause the output, "I'm fine." But it seems that some of my answers involve something else. There seems to be a difference for us in the types of responses we give that we do not need to think about, that have been ingrained in us by habit, and those we do need to think about, those that no one has told us in advance how to answer.

The idea that a computer might pass the Turing test, yet still not really think because it merely does exactly as it is programmed, is presented in a thought experiment devised by the contemporary philosopher Ned Block. Block asks us to imagine that Sam is capable of holding his own when playing any grandmaster chess player. Indeed, half of the time Sam plays chess with a grandmaster, Sam wins. Because of this, Sam passes what we can think of as the Turing test for grandmaster-level chess playing. You might think that Sam is an incredibly good chess player (just like you might think of any computer that passes the Turing test as capable of thinking). But actually, Sam doesn't even know how to play chess. Rather, the reason why he wins half the games he plays with grandmasters is because he plays as follows. In game 1, the grandmaster goes first, Sam observes what she does, and then, before making his move, he goes over to game 2 and copies the first move in game 1. Sam then observes how the grandmaster in game 2 responds to his move (which is really the move of the grandmaster in game 1), and Sam copies that move in game 2. The game proceeds like this until one of the grandmasters wins in one of the games, which ensures that Sam wins in the other. Sam's playing, it seems, would fool anyone into thinking that he is playing chess as a grandmaster, but in reality he need not even understand the game. Similarly, Block argues, a computer that is merely looking up responses in a list is not thinking.

Another contemporary philosopher, John Searle, presents an argument with a similar conclusion. Imagine that you are inside a room performing counterparts to all the relevant operations of a computer that is running a program designed to respond in a language you do not understand to questions in that language. Searle uses Chinese as the language, since he does not understand Chinese, so let us use that as well (if you understand Chinese, substitute a language you do not understand). This is how you operate the computer. When a card comes in through a slot in the box with a question on it (the input), you consult a rule book (the program), which tells you which cards with Chinese symbols you should slide out of the slot (the output). Let us say that the rule book you use is more sophisticated than any of the chat programs now in existence, so that your answers could be mistaken for a native Chinese speaker's answers. So in through the slot comes the question "Do you like to sing?" written in Chinese. You look in your rule book (which would have to be enormous) and find this question (or to be more precise, you find the lines and shapes that match the lines and shapes on your card). The book says that whenever you receive these lines and shapes, send a card out through your slot that looks like this (and here the Chinese word for "yes" is written).

The question is: Did you understand any of the conversation? Searle thinks that the answer is clearly "no"; all you did was manipulate symbols based on what they looked like, not what they meant. And since he sees no significant difference between what you were doing inside the room and what the computer did, he concludes that the computer does not understand either Chinese or any other language.

Now A.L.I.C.E.'s algorithm is more complex than the algorithm that would describe Sam's chess strategy or Searle's Chinese-language strategy. Perhaps it is true that when a computer searches through a list of questions in order to find an answer, this should not count as thinking. So, if "programming" amounts to this, then perhaps it is incompatible with thought. However, not all responses computers give are determined in advance in this way, since a computer may be created to learn from responses to its answers. A voice-recognition program, for example, does not start out knowing what you mean by everything you say, but eventually with training, it comes to understand you pretty well. But still, you might be thinking, the voice-recognition program has just been programmed to allow for further programming by its user. Once it has "learned" that when Sarah says "carrot" it should produce the word *carrot* on the screen, that is what it will always do, unless Sarah or someone else reprograms it to do something different.

What seems to be the trouble here is that voice-recognition programs, and all other programs for that matter, are not capable of freely deciding how to respond. They can't, for example, give the wrong response just because they decide to be contrary. Of course, if computers don't think merely because they are not capable of being contrary, one might justly reply, "Who needs thought?" However, there is more to this issue than that. Though it may be a good thing that computers can't be contrary, the real problem is that they do not seem to ever think for themselves, be creative, or come up with their own view on an issue. A computer that could pass the Turing test might fool us into thinking that it is thinking for itself, but it would still not be freely choosing its responses—and, therefore, one could argue, cannot think.

But what does it mean to freely choose a response? Do we freely choose our responses to questions? And if we do, how is this compatible with the laws of nature that tell us that everything is determined? The idea of free choice, however, brings us to a topic that we'll have to postpone until the later chapter on free will. So for now, let's move on to what we flagged as the second possible obstacle to computer thought: that silicon is simply not the right medium for thought.

Consider the following thought experiment. Imagine that you were going to have an operation that would replace one neuron with a computer chip. This chip would then perform the job the neuron was supposed to do when it functioned properly. Would this matter? It would seem that if the chip actually did perform the function of the neuron, you would still be able to think. Imagine also that upon recovering from the operation, you wouldn't notice any difference at all. Even imagine that due to the wonders of modern medicine, the entire operation is performed while you are conscious and that at no time do you notice that your thinking stops. As time goes on, you have more and more neural replacements, all successfully preserving neural function. Eventually, after the last operation, we can imagine that all of your brain has been replaced by wires and silicon computer chips. And still it seems to you that you are thinking. If this is so, how could being made out of flesh and blood rather than wires and silicon be relevant to whether something thinks? After all, your brain is no longer flesh and blood, yet, at least as far as you can tell, you still think. If we follow this thought experiment to its conclusion—something you may not be willing to do—then, at least one computer, that is, the one encased in your skull after the operation, thinks.

Another question to ask is whether after gradual replacement of all of your brain by silicon and wires you would still be conscious? Or more generally, can a computer be conscious? This would be relevant to the question of whether computers can think if thinking requires consciousness; if it does, and computers are not conscious, then they cannot think. But does thinking require consciousness? Most people accept that we all have thoughts that are unconscious. But could a being that was never conscious, and could never be conscious, think? Some would argue that thinking does not require consciousness, and that Searle in his "Chinese room" *is* understanding Chinese, but he is just not aware that he is understanding Chinese. Or perhaps some part of Searle is understanding Chinese—not Searle himself, but the parts of him that are involved in running the program—and those parts, while creating a conscious understanding of Chinese, are closed off to Searle's conscious mind. Can there be a part of you that is conscious but to which you have no conscious access—sort of like a fetus can be conscious inside of the mother's womb, even though the mother has no access to the consciousness? Can part of you be conscious and understand Chinese, even though your conscious mind does not? But even if thought does require consciousness, perhaps any computer complex enough to pass the Turing test would be conscious. Some of you may find it absurd to think that computers could be conscious, but as with all philosophical questions, we shouldn't arrive at conclusions before considering the arguments. Here is an argument that computers could be conscious. Again, imagine your neural replacement by silicon chips and wires. Would there be a point at which the lights go off, so to speak? Would there be a gradual dimming until there would be no inner experience left? Before we considered the idea that gradual replacement of neurons by computer chips would not eliminate thought. If we accept this, then shouldn't we arrive at the same conclusion regarding consciousness: that at the end of the operation, consciousness would be preserved?

Another consideration in favor of computer consciousness is simply the idea that it is unwarranted to deny thought or consciousness to a being just because it is made out of something different from what we are made out of. Why should the fact that a computer is made out of silicon, rather than flesh and blood, matter? Is it like denying that someone can think merely because of the color of the individual's skin or because of the individual's sex? If a person performs in a way that is consistent with thought, that person thinks regardless of skin color or sex. Similarly, as long as a computer performs in a way consistent with thought—and an indication of this is that it passes the Turing test—what reason could there be to deny any aspect of mentality to the computer?

Let's leave our discussion of computer minds with one last consideration. If computers think and are conscious, then presumably it would be immoral to destroy them or perhaps even unplug them (at least without their consent). Might we ever reach a stage in computer technology in which this is so? Could philosophical considerations reveal that computers have conscious thinking minds and thus inspire us to change the way we interact with computers? Or perhaps the revelation will come from the other direction: We will claim that computers can think when we will be morally compelled to be kind and considerate to them—to leave them plugged in, letting them go to sleep when they decide to, and, when awake, to provide them with the right sort of stimulating home environment that will let them flourish. Perhaps it will only be then that we will say, "computers think."

PROJECT SUGGESTIONS

Give A.L.I.C.E. a try online at http://www.alicebot.org/.

SUGGESTIONS FOR FURTHER READINGS

Alan Turing's engaging paper "Computing Machinery and Intelligence" was published in 1950 in the journal *Mind*. John Searle's equally engaging criticisms of artificial intelligence based on his Chinese-room argument appear in a number of his works, including his highly accessible book *Minds, Brains and Science* (Harvard University Press, 1984).

14

Mind and Meaning

"When I use a word," Humpty Dumpty said in rather
a scornful tone, "it means just what I choose it to
mean—neither more nor less."

—LEWIS CARROLL,
THROUGH THE LOOKING GLASS

"Words have no power to impress the mind without the
exquisite horror of their reality."

—EDGAR ALLAN POE

In Lewis Carroll's *Through the Looking Glass,* Humpty Dumpty
claims to be able to make words mean whatever he wants them
to. A word, he says, "means just what I choose it to mean—neither
more nor less." Is it possible to do what Humpty Dumpty says he can
do—to use a word to mean whatever you want to mean by that
word? Of course, one can, for example, say that by *and* I will mean
not, and by *blue* I will mean *green.* This, however, is not what Humpty
is claiming to be able to do, for Humpty thinks that just by the sheer
force of will he can mean whatever he likes by words. He explains to
Alice that by *impenetrability* he means "we've had enough of that
subject, and it would be just as well if you'd mention what you mean
to do next, as I suppose you don't mean to stop here all the rest of
your life." But Humpty could do this no more than I could use the
word *more* in this sentence to mean "the world has come to an end."
(Though to be fair to Humpty Dumpty, there is a sense in which

impenetrability, in the context in which he uses it, does mean what he claims it to mean, just not literally, and Alice is ever so literal-minded.)

Typically, words have a certain meaning because that is the meaning that most give to them. For example, the word *chalk* means chalk in English because most English speakers use the word *chalk* when they are describing the thing used for writing on blackboards, on the sidewalk, by schoolteachers, and so on. Or at least, that is what "descriptivists" about language claim. "Prescriptivists," on the other hand, claim that even in cases of widespread agreement, the majority can be mistaken about certain word meanings, and it is the experts who know. But neither the descriptivist nor the prescriptivist thinks that one individual can take a word that has a standard meaning and mean something utterly different by merely thinking it so, say, by thinking about blue when saying red.

To be sure, I can have a code word for something that I don't want others to know about and which I use only with my spouse. A cough, for example, can indicate that it is time to leave. Moreover, we sometimes explicitly define terms to mean what we want them to mean. For example, a mathematician could say something like: "Let us say that the *body* of a natural number is the product of its prime factors. It follows that every natural number has the same body as its square." But these examples do not show that meanings can be determined merely by thinking it so, since the examples still involve social context.

Sometimes we might slip and use a word incorrectly, and then when that incorrect usage is pointed out to us, we might say, "but that's not what I meant." For example, on an exam you might write that Julius Caesar ruled from Rheims and then try to argue with the professor afterward that you really meant to write "Rome." But in this case, it is not that your word *Rheims* meant "Rome"; that is, you would be out of place to criticize your professor for not understanding what you were saying. Rather, you really meant to say "Rome" and yet slipped and wrote something else. Or imagine a different case. Every time Joan sets off on a trip, her roommate asks her if her valise is ready to go. Joan always interprets *valise* as meaning "passport," and subsequently Joan always uses the word *valise* for passport rather than a small travel bag. But this doesn't mean that when Joan uses the word *valise* it means passport; rather, it would seem to show that Joan is simply using the term *valise* incorrectly.

Sometimes you might also use words to make someone think that you are saying something quite different from what your words are typically thought to mean. For example, if you were to shiver and rub your hands together while saying "piano, piano," this might make a non–English speaker think that *piano* means cold. But although this may be the meaning you intended, it would seem that it is not what your words mean. The contemporary philosopher, John Searle, presents a vivid illustration of this phenomenon. Searle asks us to imagine that he is an American soldier during World War II who has just been captured by Italians. He wants to try to convince the Italians that he is a German soldier. So he recites the only German sentence he knows—"Kennst du das Land wo die Zitronen blühen"—a line from a poem he memorized in his high school German class. By doing this, he convinces the Italians that he is a German soldier. But, as Searle points out, no matter how hard he wills it, the German sentence doesn't mean "I am a German soldier." Rather, according to Searle, it has its conventional meaning, which is "Knowest thou the land where the lemon trees bloom?" And this is true, whether or not it has the intended effect on the listeners.

It seems, then, that Humpty Dumpty is wrong: You can't make words mean whatever you want them to mean. When it comes to language, it seems that what is going on in your mind when you speak does not fully determine what you mean. Words have certain conventional meanings, and no matter how much I might think that I can mean *bird* by my utterance of *butterfly,* when I say, "butterflies have beaks," the meaning of this sentence is in some sense out of my control.

An influential thought experiment by the contemporary philosopher Hilary Putnam takes a different route to this conclusion. Imagine that far off in a distant galaxy there is a planet very much like our planet. There are trees, oceans, people, and animals that, if we were to visit this planet, would look just like the trees, oceans, people, and animals here on earth. In fact, this planet seems to be identical in every way to earth. For example, on this planet, there is a town just like the one you live in and a student just like you reading a book just like this, seated in a room just like the room you happen to be seated in now. Although there are no apparent differences between our planet and this faraway planet, which we can call "Twin Earth," a closer examination of Twin Earth would show that it is not exactly like earth, since the stuff in the lakes, rivers, oceans, and reservoirs, though it superficially looks and behaves just like water, is not composed of H_2O. Rather, it has a very complex chemical composition that is unlike anything on earth, and which for simplicity we can abbreviate as "XYZ."

According to Putnam, the stuff in the lakes, rivers, reservoirs, and so forth on Twin Earth is not water because water, on Putnam's view, is H_2O, while the stuff on Twin Earth is XYZ. Of course, the Twin Earthlings refer to the clear stuff that they drink as *water,* but they do not mean what we mean when we say *water.* Rather, according to Putnam, the two words (*water* as uttered on earth, and *water* as uttered on Twin Earth) are homonyms, for when the Twin Earthlings utter the word *water,* what they mean is XYZ, while what we mean by *water* is H_2O.

That the Twin Earthlings' utterance of *water* means something different from our utterance of *water* shows, according to Putnam, that something outside of the mind or brain seems to at least in part determine what we (or they, or anyone at all) mean by our words. To see why this is so, imagine going back to a time before 1781 so that neither the Twin Earthlings nor we have any idea about the chemical composition of the stuff in rivers, lakes, and so on. Jill and her twin on Twin Earth could have learned about the world in the same way, and thus presumably would have identically neurological configurations; yet even so, Jill and Twin Jill would mean different things by *water,* since, according to Putnam, the term didn't change its meaning after 1781. Rather, *water* is what is thought to be one of many "natural kind terms": It means that stuff (imagine pointing to water right now), whatever it happens to be. If it turns out by some strange fluke that water here on earth is not H_2O, then our word *water,* it is thought, actually doesn't mean H_2O. But given that water is H_2O, *water* has the meaning H_2O. So, Humpty Dumpty is wrong: I can't choose to make my words mean whatever I want them to, since sometimes the meaning of my words depends on things out in the world that aren't under my control, such as the chemical composition of water. Or, in Putnam's words, "cut the pie any way you like, 'meanings' just ain't in the head."

But let's move from thinking about the meaning of words to thinking about the mind. The Twin Earth thought experiment is relevant to philosophy of mind, since it seems that what goes for meanings also goes for beliefs; that is, there is a sense in which not only what you mean by words, but also what you believe, is not entirely up to you. Jill here on earth will, upon pouring a glass of water, believe that there is water in her glass, but Jill's twin on Twin Earth will not believe this. Twin Jill will have a belief that she would describe as the belief that water is in her glass; however, if *water* here and *water* on Twin Earth are homonyms, then although Twin Jill believes truly that what is in her glass is what she calls *water*, she doesn't believe that what we call *water* is in her glass. Yet, Jill here on earth does believe this. Indeed, if Twin Jill believed that water, that is, H_2O, was in her glass, her belief would be false. So it seems that despite the fact that Jill and Twin Jill are identical in terms of everything that is going on in their heads, they have different beliefs: Jill has beliefs about water (that is, H_2O); Twin Jill does not.

The view that what we believe depends on factors external to us is called "externalism," or "content externalism" (the "content" of a belief being what that thought is about; for example, if I believe that it is raining, the content of my belief is that it is raining). Is this view plausible? It seems that once we accept Putnam's argument that meanings are not in the head, then it is rather a quick move to see why beliefs are not also. So if we want to question externalism, we should go back to Putnam's argument that what we mean depends on external factors.

Putnam claims that there can be two individuals who are internally identical yet mean different things when they say, for example, "water is wet" or "I would like a glass of water," since if one is on earth where water is H_2O and another is on Twin Earth where water is XYZ, when the individual on earth says, "water is wet," she means H_2O is wet, but when the individual on Twin Earth says this, she means that XYZ is wet. Now, is this plausible? It is often pointed out that Jill on earth and Twin Jill on Twin Earth cannot actually be internally identical, since adults on earth are typically sixty percent water, and thus Jill will be sixty percent H_2O, and Twin Jill will be sixty percent XYZ. This problem is typically ignored in the thought experiment, however, since this difference between Jill and Twin Jill is thought to be irrelevant to what they mean by their words. Moreover, the thought experiment could be reformulated in terms of something that does not occur in the human body, such as petroleum. When Jill believes that the price of a barrel of petroleum has risen, she has a belief about petroleum. But Twin Jill, Putnam could argue, would not have this belief, since on her planet there is only Twin Petroleum, which is very similar to petroleum—it is used to make gasoline and jet fuel, for example—yet has a different underlying chemical structure. In line with Putnam's thought experiment, Jill and Twin Jill would mean different things when they talk about petroleum, even though they are internally identical. A deeper issue is whether Putnam is correct in claiming that water is necessarily H_2O. In other words, is Putnam correct in claiming that anything that is not H_2O, such as the stuff on Twin Earth, is not water? Most philosophers think that Putnam is correct in claiming this, but others see it as an open question. Putnam sets up his thought experiment so that the reader is carried along into thinking that this must be so; he doesn't even refer to the stuff on Twin Earth as "*water*" but rather as "*twater*." But must we think that the stuff on Twin Earth is not water? Perhaps water just comes in different forms. If in the highly unlikely event we discovered some place like Twin Earth, would we say that what they have there is not water, or just that they have a different kind of water? It seems we could go either way. Those who disagree with Putnam about the nature of water think that this is what we should say about the stuff on Twin Earth as well. If the stuff on Twin Earth is water, however, Jill and Twin Jill mean the same thing when they say "water is wet," and correlatively both believe that water is wet. If this is so, Putnam's attempt to show that what you mean by your words is in part determined by factors external to you does not succeed.

One might even ask whether it is correct to say that here on earth water is H_2O. Water may be composed in part by H_2O, but the stuff in lakes, rivers, drinking faucets, and even bottles of "pure mountain spring water" is not just H_2O, yet we call all that stuff *water*. It has even been said that pound for pound, newborn babies have just as much H_2O in them as the stuff one finds in the Great Salt Lake, yet we call the stuff in the Great Salt Lake, but not babies, *water*.

Whether or not these considerations refute Putnam, there are other reasons for thinking that we cannot mean whatever we want to by our words. One of these reasons is simply that words are given meaning in a social context. You might think that the word *cat* means what I think of as a dog, but this doesn't make your utterance of the word *cat* mean dog.

Such considerations form the basis for another argument for externalism, that is, for the view that what we believe depends on factors external to us. The argument is that of the contemporary philosopher Tyler Burge, and it goes like this. Aunt Edna, let us say, has arthritis in her fingers. It has been bothering her for years, never getting any better, though never getting worse either. Lately, however, she's been worried because she's been having some aches and pains in her thigh. Not knowing that arthritis is a disease of the joints that does not occur in muscles, she believes that she has very painful arthritis in her thigh muscle. Now imagine, however, someone who is internally like Aunt Edna in every way. She also has had arthritis in her fingers for years, and now thinks that it has moved to her thigh. However, this other Aunt Edna, let's call her Aunt Ande, lives in a community in which the term *arthritis* is thought of as a disease of both the joints and the muscles. Aunt Edna and Aunt Ande are alike in all internal respects—same aches, same physiology, same processes going on in their heads. Yet, according to Burge, their beliefs differ: Aunt Edna believes that she has painful arthritis in her thigh, and that she has had arthritis in her fingers for years; Aunt Ande, however, has none of these beliefs. Even though they would express their beliefs in the same way, they don't actually have the same beliefs. Rather, Aunt Ande has beliefs about something different, something that can afflict muscles as well as joints. Thus, concludes Burge, what you believe depends at least in part on the social community in which you live.

Now, here again, there are questions one should ask. For example, some ask whether it is right to say that Aunt Edna (in our linguistic community) actually believes that she has arthritis in her thigh. She might use the word *arthritis* to describe what it is that she believes, but is this the correct description of her belief? If arthritis is a disease of the joints, then doesn't she actually believe that she has some other illness? Another question is what implications externalism has for whether even you yourself can know what you believe, for if your belief depends on factors outside of you of which you are unaware, you might very well be unaware of what it is you believe. But isn't each individual the best authority for what he or she believes?

Some argue for an even more radical form of externalism that holds that not only is what you believe determined in part by factors external to you, but also some aspects of your mind itself are external, in the sense of not being inside your skin. For example, your cell phone most likely carries numerous phone numbers. Do you know these phone numbers? Well, if my number was in your phone and I asked you if you knew my number, you would say, "yes," even if you needed to look it up. So, is there a sense then in which the contents of your phone are actually part of your mind? I will leave you to ponder these aspects of externalism. Are you sympathetic to any form of it? Or would you, perhaps, rather go back and side with Humpty Dumpty?

SUGGESTIONS FOR FURTHER READING

Putnam argues for his view that what we mean by the words we use depends on how things are in the world in "The Meaning of 'Meaning,'" and Burge presents his argument for content externalism in his paper "Individualism and the Mental." Both of these papers can be found in numerous anthologies in philosophy of mind, including Chalmers's *Philosophy of Mind: Classical and Contemporary Readings*. Searle discusses his German soldier example in his book *Speech Acts: An Essay in the Philosophy of Language* (Cambridge University Press, 1969). And if you've never read Lewis Carroll's *Through the Looking Glass,* or only did so as a young child, you are in for a treat, as it is brimming with philosophical ideas.

15

Consciousness

The highest activities of consciousness have their origins
in physical occurrences of the brain just as the loveliest
melodies are not too sublime to be expressed by notes.

—SOMERSET MAUGHAM,

A WRITER'S NOTEBOOK (1949)

"Consciousness is what makes the mind-body problem
really intractable."

—THOMAS NAGEL,

"WHAT IT IS LIKE TO BE A BAT" (1974)

D irect your attention to your experience of the page before you:
its contours, its texture, its color, the rustling sound it makes
when turned. What is it like for you to experience the page in this
way? Perhaps before I asked you to focus on the sound the page
makes when turned, you weren't fully aware of it. But now it seems
fully present to your mind. You are now *conscious* of the page.

But what was going on before you focused on the sound? Were
you not conscious of the sound? The sound waves were still entering
your ears. So there is a sense in which you were hearing the sound
before you turned your attention to it. But should we say that you
were consciously hearing the sound? Or consider the feeling of the
chair you are sitting on. Now that you focus on it, you are conscious
of the feeling of pressure against your body. However, did you feel
the pressure even before you focused on it? Or think about the

position and movements of your limbs. If you've managed to turn the pages of this book (or push the page down button, as the case may be), you must have a sense of where your hands are and how they are moving. And when you focus on their movements, you become consciously aware of them. But what was going on before you focused on them? Was the feeling of movement entirely unconscious?

Although there is a sense in which we all know exactly what consciousness is, philosophers disagree adamantly about how to explain it. Is consciousness is a physical phenomenon? How much of our mental life is conscious? Does consciousness have a function, and if it does, what is it? Are we, as limited creatures, even capable of understanding the nature of consciousness and how the brain gives rise to consciousness (if, indeed, it does)? "Consciousness" as Thomas Nagel says, "is what makes the mind-body problem really intractable." And the reason for this is that it seems incomprehensible how something entirely physical, such as the brain, can give rise to conscious experience. Neuroscience can investigate what neural structures subserve conscious experience, but it is utterly mysterious how processes in the brain can account for the way the world seems to me in all its variegated ways.

Take a moment, now, and try to become conscious of your consciousness. What do you find? What does it feel like to be conscious? Are you experiencing a whirr of thoughts? Is your mind filled with images? Do you have an awareness of where you are in space? The process of introspecting and reporting on what you find in your own experience is called "phenomenology," and in order to think about consciousness, we rely not only on neurology, which may be able to reveal the underlying neural structure of consciousness, but also on phenomenology, which reveals the experience itself. Introspect, and you find what it is that a theory of consciousness aims to explain.

Introspection is something we can all readily do, but the process is not as simple as it may seem at first. Phenomenology is a thorny endeavor for at least two reasons. One is that introspection is not entirely trustworthy. For example, you might introspect and find what you take to be sadness, when in reality you are just feeling tired. So we need to proceed cautiously. But even when we proceed cautiously, the results should be thought of as defeasible, that is, as tentative and liable to be given up if contradicted by other results. For example, they should be given up if we find experiments performed by neuroscientists or psychologists that contradict results obtained from introspection. But often in thinking about consciousness, introspection is the only tool we have.

The other reason phenomenology is tricky is that sometimes in studying consciousness, the very process of introspection can change it. For example, if you try to focus on your paper cut to determine what it feels like, you might become aware of its sting, of which you were previously unaware. And most of us can attest to the powers of distraction for pain relief or, even more effective, for the relief of an itch. (Oddly enough, however, although distraction often works to alleviate pain, I have heard that intense focusing on the pain can be palliative as well.) What are we to do about the fact that introspection can change the quality of what you are trying to introspect? The only thing it seems we can do is to be aware of it and try to adjust our views accordingly.

People and animals have a point of view or a perspective on the world, whereas rocks and chairs do not. When you are awake, there is something it feels like for you to be awake. There is something it feels like to be you. In contrast to this, there is nothing it feels like for a rock to be a rock or a sock to be a sock (fortunately, too, since my old socks replete with holes would feel pretty terrible if they were conscious). So I am conscious while my socks are not. The type of consciousness we attribute to people and animals is what the contemporary philosopher David Rosenthal dubs "creature consciousness." And when I said that anyone who is reading this book is conscious, the type of consciousness I had in mind was creature consciousness.

Philosophers often assume that if someone is passed out or receiving general anesthesia or in deep sleep, then that person is not conscious. And indeed, the notion of creature consciousness is often explained by contrasting it with sleep or general anesthesia. But how, exactly, to draw the line between being conscious and not being conscious is not entirely straightforward. For example, what happens when you fall asleep? Should we say that when you are asleep you are not conscious? In dreams we have experiences: A dream can be vivid, beautiful, frightening, or pleasurable. And it seems that if a person is having experiences, that person must be conscious in some sense. However, there does seem to be a sort of blankness to dreamless sleep; dreamless sleep doesn't seem to involve experiences or feel like anything. Nonetheless, there is a significant difference between being in a dreamless sleep and being comatose, or unconscious. Someone in a coma will not be roused by an alarm clock, but even in a dreamless sleep you can become conscious of your alarm. Or can you? Do you hear your alarm when you are in deep sleep, or does the alarm rouse you from a deep sleep into a lighter sleep and then you hear the alarm? But whether you hear it or not during a dreamless sleep, it will, nonetheless, rouse you; in a coma, you will not even be roused by an alarm. And if you can be so readily roused, is it right to say that you were not conscious? And how are we to describe your ability to not fall off the bed? Are you conscious of your body's position on the bed? Or do you lose this consciousness during deep sleep, but since you do not typically move around during deep sleep, it doesn't matter?

Undergoing general anesthesia is more clearly a case of loss of consciousness than is undergoing sleep. However, occasionally a patient will have explicit memories of what was said during an operation or, even worse, though fortunately very rarely, will recall horrific pain. This may not be significant, however, to the discussion of how to demarcate creature consciousness from creature unconsciousness, as it is generally assumed that intraoperative awareness is due to too little anesthesia. However, there is currently much research on this, as it is not fully understood.

A more common occurrence, however, is for patients to have implicit memories of what was said. For example, if a recording of the word *pension* was played during the operation, the patient will be more likely to fill in the word stem "pen__" with "sion" than with "tagon" or "ny." But does this mean that the patient was conscious of these sounds during the operation? Or would a better explanation of this be that even when we are unconscious, we can process information that later affects such guesses? In thinking about the distinction between being conscious and not being conscious, an interesting case to ponder is somnambulism, or sleepwalking. Sleepwalkers can do a surprising number of things. With glassy eyes staring wide open, a sleepwalker might walk downstairs, move furniture, or even go for a drive. On the one hand, it would seem impossible to do all this without being conscious. On the other hand, upon waking, the sleepwalker will have no recollection of the events, indicating that he or she lacked consciousness. Moreover, it is sometimes very difficult to rouse a sleepwalker. (A common misconception is that it is dangerous to wake a sleepwalker; it is not dangerous, but it can be difficult.) Somnambulism occurs during deep sleep, but it is an atypical case of deep sleep where one moves around a lot and involves brainwaves that are characteristic of deep sleep and also ones that are characteristic of periods of wakefulness. How are we to classify somnambulism, or sleepwalking? Is the sleepwalker conscious or not? Or do we need to say that the sleepwalker is partially conscious and partially not conscious?

I can be conscious of a color, a thought, a rabbit, or a sunrise. But we also talk about being conscious *that* something is so and so. You might, for example, not only be conscious of your friend's new chartreuse hat, but also be conscious that your friend has a new chartreuse hat. What is the difference between what we might call "consciousness of" and "consciousness that"? The basic idea is that sometimes you can be conscious of something without knowing what that thing is. For example, if you do not know what color chartreuse is, you could still be conscious *of* the color of your friend's chartreuse hat. You wouldn't, however, be conscious *that,* or aware *that,* the hat is chartreuse. Or say that you look at a painting of a flock of seventy-four birds. You will be conscious of the seventy-four birds even if you are not aware of how many there are, but in order to be conscious that there are seventy-four birds, you would need to count them.

So there seems to be a distinction between being conscious of something and being conscious that something is so. But if these are two different kinds of conscious experiences, then it would seem that they could at least possibly come apart, that is, that you could have one type without the other. Can you be conscious of something without being conscious that it is one way or another? Can you just be aware of the color chartreuse without being aware that it is chartreuse or even that it is some color or other? Or is it that every time you are conscious of something, you are also conscious that it is a certain way. For example, when you are conscious of the color of your friend's hat even when you do not know what color chartreuse is, you still may be conscious that the hat is a pale, yellowish green. And when you are conscious of the flock of birds, you might not be conscious that there are seventy-four birds, but you still may be conscious that there are a great many birds upon the canvas. Does this mean that in order to be conscious of the birds you must be conscious that they are one way or another? Could it be that all consciousness involves consciousness that something is a certain way?

In addition to saying that a person is conscious, we also say that people have certain conscious experiences, beliefs, thoughts, and so forth; you might be consciously perceiving a chartreuse hat, or consciously experiencing pain, or consciously thinking about going swimming. Rosenthal calls this "state consciousness" because there is a certain *state* you are in that is conscious: your perception of a chartreuse hat, your experience of pain, or your thought about going swimming.

We can better understand what it means for these states to be conscious by contrasting them with unconscious states. Most people accept the idea that some of what is in your mind is not currently present to consciousness. For example, you believe that $2 + 2 = 4$. And you believed this a minute ago, even though you weren't consciously thinking about it. So it seems that unconscious beliefs are commonplace. Moreover, since Sigmund Freud introduced the idea that unconscious desires, beliefs, fears, and so forth can influence your behavior, many people accept that some of your mental life may be presently inaccessible to you, though, perhaps, a therapist or a friend could bring you to become aware of this aspect of your mind. For example, after hearing the news about a tragic mountain climbing accident, you might feel fear at the prospect of going mountain climbing again. However, since you love mountain climbing and do not want to think of yourself as someone who lets fears like these get in your way, the fear does not raise to the level of consciousness. Nevertheless, your best friend and mountain climbing buddy notices that you have been avoiding her at all costs. She suspects it has to do with you wanting to avoid being asked to go climbing, and when she confronts you with this, you realize she is right. Your fear prior to this confrontation was, arguably, both genuine and not conscious.

But what about unconscious perceptions? For example, since I live across from Trinity Church in lower Manhattan, I often am aware of the church bells chiming out the quarter hours. That is, I often consciously perceive the bells chiming. But sometimes I do not notice them at all. As I am sure that they are nonetheless ringing every fifteen minutes, and that if I were to focus on them I would hear them, is it right to say that in this situation I am "unconsciously perceiving" the bells? Or consider proprioception—the sense by which we acquire information, via receptors in the joints, tendons, ligaments, muscles, and skin, about the positions and movements of our own bodies. If you proprioceptively focus on the angle of your left knee, your proprioception will be conscious. But most of the time you seem to know where your limbs are unconsciously. Moreover, images flashed too quickly to be consciously registered can nonetheless leave an impression on you, influencing your later behavior. It seems that we should say that perception occurs in these cases, just not conscious perception.

Can we also say that you can be either conscious of pain or not conscious of pain? That is, can we say that pains can occur unnoticed? Pains, quite unfortunately, sometimes do seem to be fully present to one's consciousness. But must they be? Perhaps you have performed on stage or participated in an athletic game where during the event you failed to notice the terrible shoulder pain you had been having all day. As soon as the event was over, however, you noticed it again. What is going on here? Were you actually in pain during the performance or game even though you didn't notice it, or did your pain vanish during the performance or game and come back after you finished?

Unconscious thought is easier to accept than unconscious pain. Right now, I'm consciously thinking about how to present these ideas; my thoughts—more so than the humid New York City weather, or the background conversation in the café in which I am working—are really present to my mind, although this can easily change. Indeed, as soon as I wrote about the weather and the background conversation, both of those things became more prominent in my mind. But while it seems that unnoticed thoughts should still count as thoughts, it is not at all clear whether unnoticed pains (if we should call them that) should count as pains. Some of what is at stake is terminology. That is, we need to decide whether we should call both the shoulder pain you feel before the event and the state you are in during the event "pain." This does not mean, however, that it is entirely arbitrary whether pain, in order to count as real pain, must be conscious, since what we are doing here as philosophers is trying to determine whether there are good reasons to call both states *pain states* or whether we should reserve that term only for conscious states. What might these reasons be? If we were to find that the neural mechanisms underlying both states were significantly similar, would we count both as "pain"? Or do we need to find that both states also involve the brain state that underlies awareness, assuming there is such a thing?

An unusual phenomenon that some see as an example of unconscious perception is "blindsight." Blindsight is caused by damage to the visual cortex that results in blindness in a certain part of the visual field that allows, oddly enough, for some visual functioning. Individuals with blindsight claim to see nothing, yet if pressed to guess what they are seeing, will typically guess correctly. For example, if an experimenter presents a card with an O on it to an individual with blindsight and asks whether there is an X or an O on the card, the subject will report that he or she cannot tell. However, if told to guess, the subject—after protesting that he or she can see nothing—will guess O. Some think that the best way to describe what is going on is that individuals with blindsight can perceive the X or O, only not consciously.

But could there be a sense in which individuals with blindsight are conscious of what they are perceiving? The contemporary philosopher Ned Block has argued that there exists a distinction between two kinds of state consciousness. One kind, what he calls "access consciousness," is characterized by its accessibility to you: You can readily report it ("I'm in pain now") and act on it (move away from the painful stimuli). The other type of state consciousness, what he calls "phenomenal consciousness," is characterized by feeling a certain way to you. The pain is phenomenally conscious if you feel it; a visual experience of seeing red is phenomenally conscious if the redness appears to you in a certain way or, as philosophers say, if there is "something it is like" to see red. Typically, these two kinds of consciousness go together. When I hear a siren, not only does it sound like something to me (this is the phenomenal aspect), but I will also look up from what I am doing, or wait at the crosswalk, or some such thing (in this way it is accessible to me).

In order to substantiate that there is such a distinction, Block suggests that these two kinds of consciousness could, in principle, come apart. And he thinks that blindsight at least suggests that someone can have access consciousness without having phenomenal consciousness. Blindsight, however, is not really an example of access consciousness, as Block himself points out, since individuals with blindsight do not readily report or act on their perception. Rather, their responses to questions about the images they "see" need to be solicited. Nonetheless, Block thinks that actual cases of blindsight suggest that it is possible for there to be someone with what he calls "super-blindsight," a condition that would allow an individual to accurately and spontaneously respond to questions as well as behave appropriately with respect to things of which the individual is not phenomenally conscious. The individual with super-blindsight has no visual experience of the world, and yet is able to get around, follow written directions, bicycle down the road, and so on, without any problem. This conceptual possibility, argues Block, illustrates the distinction between the two forms of consciousness.

But does it? Is such a scenario even conceptually possible? In particular, when we imagine the super-blindsighter, are we imagining someone with conscious perception of what he or she sees? If not, the thought experiment does not support the idea that we may have two different forms of consciousness. Moreover, even if we can make conceptual sense of Block's thought experiment, it is not clear what it shows about us. Perhaps there could be some form of consciousness that does not facilitate reports about it and actions based on it. But why think that we have such a form of consciousness?

Another question that arises about the nature of consciousness is more basic: state consciousness or creature consciousness? (Recall that "state consciousness" applies to perceptions, sensations, and thoughts that are conscious, while creature consciousness applies to a person when we say that a person is conscious as opposed to being in a deep coma.) Can a person be conscious, for example, awake and alert, without being in any conscious states: no pains, no itches, no experiences of color or sound? I have had students tell me that during meditation it is possible to attain a state in which you are not conscious of anything at all, and yet you are still conscious. Are my students who have had this sort of experience none-theless having a conscious experience of silence? This seems to be a rather desperate maneuver to save the view that every time you are conscious you are in some conscious state or another. Probably a better tack to take if you are committed to the idea that whenever a person is conscious, that person is always having a conscious experience is to question the results of introspection: Perhaps introspection is wrong when it tells us that we are conscious but not conscious of anything (or at best conscious of silence).

Putting aside the question of whether someone can be conscious without having any conscious experiences, let us ask whether someone can have conscious experiences without being conscious. That is, is state consciousness possible without creature consciousness? State con-sciousness without creature consciousness seems harder to accept, for it would seem that you need to be conscious in order to have a conscious experience. Indeed, how would we ever know about conscious pain—that is, pain that feels painful—in someone who is unconscious? If you are unconscious, you can't say, "I'm in pain," and you might not remember being in pain. So what could provide evidence for the existence of conscious sensations in someone who is unconscious?

If you think that you are unconscious when dreaming, perhaps dreams could be an example of this. Dreams have a certain feeling to them. The colors, the sounds, and the emotions in dreams all have a certain feeling to them; there is, in Thomas Nagel's words, "something it is like" to dream. Yet, if we are unconscious while dreaming, then dreams are conscious experiences we have when we are unconscious.

Most people, however, would prefer to say that we are conscious during dreams and so would reject this as an example of state consciousness without creature consciousness. A better example would be the phenomenon of intraoperative pain, which I mentioned earlier. Conscious pain during general anesthesia would seem to be an example of a conscious sensation in someone who is unconscious. The cause of intraoperative pain, however, is usually thought to be insufficient sedation. So it seems that the patient is not actually unconscious. However, if it such pain could occur even with sufficient sedation—sufficient, that is, for the purpose of making the patient unconscious—we would seem to have an example of state consciousness without creature consciousness.

Rosenthal has argued that in order for a pain to be conscious, we have to be aware of the pain; I have a conscious pain, for example, if I am in pain and I have a thought about it. And so if we are to have pain during sleep, it would not be conscious pain, on Rosenthal's view, unless we in some way are aware of the pain. Not any sort of awareness will do, however. You might have repressed a desire to go to art school because your mother wants so desperately for you to be a doctor. Your psychoanalyst, however, tells you that you actually do have this desire. Your psychoanalyst could be right: You might have this desire. And in telling you this, she makes you aware of the desire; but because it is so deeply repressed, the desire remains unconscious. So becoming aware of a mental state through being told about it by someone else might not bring that mental state to consciousness. Rather, according to Rosenthal, you need to become aware of it directly. And when you do become aware of belief, thought, desire, pain, or other mental state directly, that mental state becomes a conscious mental state.

Is this what makes your beliefs, thoughts, desires, pains, and other mental states conscious? Defenders of the view think that ultimately the answer will be determined empirically. Science will prove the theory correct or incorrect. Or at least they believe that the question can only ultimately be settled empirically; whether it will ever be settled is something those of us alive today probably will never know.

SUGGESTIONS FOR FURTHER READING

The anthology *The Nature of Consciousness: Philosophical Debates,* edited by Ned Block, Owen Flanagan, and Güven Güzeldere (MIT Press, 1998), contains numerous fascinating articles on consciousness, including Fred Dretske's paper "Conscious Experience" in which he argues that one can be conscious of something without being conscious that it is a thing of its kind, David Rosenthal's paper "A Theory of Consciousness" where he presents the distinction between creature consciousness and state consciousness, and Ned Block's paper "A Confusion about the Function of Consciousness" in which he distinguishes access consciousness from phenomenal consciousness.

16

The "Body" Side of the Mind-Body Problem

The physical world is meaningless tonight
And there is no other.
—WALLACE STEVENS, "JOUGA" (1923)

Matter has become as ghostly as anything in a spiritualist's séance.
—BERTRAND RUSSELL,
THE ANALYSIS OF MATTER (1927)

The mind-body problem, as we have been exploring it, is the problem of understanding the relation between mind and body, or, as it is sometimes put, it is the problem of understanding how the mind fits into the physical world. But although most philosophers of mind focus, reasonably enough, on understanding mind, we should not altogether ignore the body, or more broadly, the physical world. We should not do this because in order to understand even the question "Is the mind physical?" we need some understanding of what the physical is, that is, some understanding of the body side of the mind-body problem.

Here are two philosophy students arguing about whether the mind is physical:

A: There is no question about it, the mind, along with everything else in this world, is entirely physical.

B: How could you say that? Physics goes only so far. It provides an account of particles and forces, but the world of mind is entirely out of the physical realm altogether.

How are we to resolve the debate between A and B? An important preliminary step in resolving this debate in particular, and the debate between physicalists and antiphysicalists more generally, is to make it clear what each means by the term *physical*. For example, perhaps A thinks of the physical realm as the realm of spatially extended entities and so is merely claiming that the mind is spatially extended. And perhaps B thinks of the physical realm as the realm of entities, properties, and forces of physics (quarks, leptons, the strong force, the weak force, and so forth) as well as anything that can be fully explained in terms of such entities. If this were the case, they could both be correct. This would happen if, say, the mind were spatially extended but not even in principle explainable in terms of the entities, properties, and forces of physics. But if they could both be correct, then A and B were not really arguing in the first place, but merely talking past each other.

What, then, is the relevant notion of the physical that creates genuine debates over the nature of the mind? Oddly enough, even though the concept of the physical enters into almost all the debates over the mind-body problem, it is rarely defined explicitly. Moreover, doing so is not as straightforward as one might think. Let us look, then, not at the nature of mind, but rather at the nature of body—an investigation into what I call the "body problem."

One way of trying to grasp what we mean by the physical in asking whether the mind is physical is to try to identify its contrast, namely, the nonphysical or immaterial, since if we have a grasp of the nonphysical, we can say that the physical is just not that. Well, then, what is the nonphysical? The stock example of a nonphysical entity is some kind of ghost. For example, it is sometimes claimed that to be a physicalist, that is, to claim that everything is physical, is to at least deny that there are ghosts. But what are ghosts, and why, if they were to exist, would they be nonphysical? It might be said that ghosts are immaterial beings. Perhaps so, but since *immaterial* and *nonphysical* are for the most part used interchangeably, this type of definition does not help us to understand what it is that physicalists (those who deny that there is anything immaterial or nonphysical) actually deny.

What is it about ghosts that are supposed to make them, if they were to exist, nonphysical? Ghosts are supposed to be able to do strange things and have odd properties. For example, ghosts, it is thought, pass through walls without disturbing them. But passing through walls without disturbing them is something certain particles called "neutrinos" do all the time. Yet we wouldn't want to classify neutrinos as nonphysical. Could it be that what is spooky about ghosts is that they have no mass? This seems unlikely as well, since photons have no mass yet do not seem to pose a problem for physicalism. Perhaps the odd thing about ghosts is that they do not take up space. But if taking up no space shows that something is nonphysical, point particles (if they exist) would have to be classified as nonphysical. Yet physicalists, I take it, would not accept this view. So to identify the nonphysical with the ghostly does not help us to identify the physical.

To drive this point home, consider what would happen if we were to find that ghosts really and truly do exist. Would we still want to call them nonphysical? It seems that much of the motivation for identifying the nonphysical with spooks comes from our conviction that ghosts do not exist. But once they are in the world, why should we think of them as nonphysical?

If the physical doesn't exclude ghosts, what does it exclude? If you are a physicalist, then everything is physical, so there is no contrasting class. But even a physicalist needs to be able to state what it is that, if it were to exist, would count as nonphysical. If this cannot be done, physicalism would seem to be a view that no one could possibly disagree with, since everyone accepts that if we merely define the physical so that any actual or possible thing counts as physical, nothing can be nonphysical. So something more needs to be said.

Perhaps physicalists want to deny the existence of a substance that is completely different in kind from physical substance. But what does this view amount to? What does it mean to deny that there are more kinds of substances than physical substance? It is commonly thought that there are many different kinds of elementary particles. Yet this type of variety, it would seem, is perfectly consistent with physicalism. Perhaps the idea is that whether only one basic particle exists, say, strings, or it turns out that in addition to strings there are also, say, microsized Ferris wheels, physicalism holds that everything nonbasic is composed of the same kind, or kinds, of basic particles.

But even this does not quite capture what seems to be at issue between supporters and detractors of physicalism. The reason is that some evidence indicates that what physicists call "dark matter" is composed entirely of axions, hypothetical new elementary particles. Yet dark matter is no threat to physicalism. So the simple notion of *stuff of a different kind* does not provide us with a notion of nonphysical. But what, then, does?

Philosophers commonly answer this question by deferring to the physicists. The physical is said to be whatever the physicist, or more precisely, the particle physicist, tells us exists (what we might now think of as quarks and leptons, as well as the exchange particles, gluons, gravitons, and so on). And the nonphysical is whatever remains, if there is anything. On this view, physicalists claim that physics provides us with an exhaustive and exclusive line to all reality. Here is a straightforward answer to the body problem, but one that is too simple, since most philosophers believe that things like rocks, tables, and chairs are just as physical as quarks, leptons, and gluons.

To be sure, whether or not we should say that the physical is only what the physicists take as fundamental is partially a terminological issue. I was present at a seminar once where a debate erupted about whether rocks are physical, with the professor insisting that no matter what else is true, rocks are physical, while the student kept replying that rocks are clearly not physical. What was going on, though I'm not sure if either ever made his position clear to the other, was that the student was using the term *physical* to refer to the fundamental entities of physics while the professor was using the term broadly.

But while the question of whether we should reserve the name *physical* for just the fundamental constituents of reality rather than using it more broadly *is* terminological, the question of how many layers of reality to countenance is not. Since most physicalists allow for not only the smallest stuff, but also for atoms, molecules, rocks, and galaxies, the leave-it-to-the-physicists approach is usually amended to the view that the physical world is the world of the fundamental particles, forces, laws, and so forth, *as well as* whatever depends on this fundamental stuff.

But how are we to characterize the fundamental level—what is often referred to as the "microphysical"? If physicalism is the view, for example, that everything is composed of microphysical phenomena, we need an understanding of what counts as microphysical phenomena in order to understand physicalism. Typically, one thinks of microphysical phenomena as that which is described by the most recent microphysics. But if the physical is defined once and for all in terms of the microphysics we have today, and a new particle is discovered next week, then the particle will not be physical. This is a consequence most philosophers want to avoid. But if the physical is not to be defined in terms of not-current microphysics, what else could the microphysical be?

A well-known dilemma was presented by Carl Hempel (1905–1997) for those attempting to define the physical in reference to microphysics. On the one hand, we cannot define the physical in terms of current microphysics, since today's microphysics is probably neither entirely true (some of our theories may look as wrong-headed to future generations as phlogiston theory looks to us now) nor complete (more remains to be explained). On the other hand, if we take microphysics to be some future unspecified theory, the claim that the mind is physical is vague, since we currently have no idea of what that theory might be. Faced with this dilemma, what is a physicalist to do?

Some try to take the middle road, explaining the "microphysical" by claiming that the microphysics at issue is going to be similar to current physics, yet improved. But in what respect will this future microphysics be like current microphysics? And in what respect will it be improved? Since these questions are usually not addressed (save, of course, for the implication that it will be similar enough to be intelligible yet different enough to be true), it seems that Hempel's dilemma recurs for these compromise views, since the theory in question will be false if it is significantly similar to current physics, and if it is not, we are left with no clear notion of the physical.

Taking the first horn of Hempel's dilemma, that is, defining the physical in terms of current microphysics, does not provide us with a comfortable solution to the body problem. For it is rather awkward to hold a theory that one knows is false. But does taking the second horn allow us to fare any better? Many philosophers think so and define the physical accordingly. For example, David Armstrong explicitly tells us that when he says "physical properties," he is not talking about the properties specified by current physics, but rather "whatever set of properties the physicist in the end will appeal to." Similarly, Frank Jackson holds that the physical facts encompass "everything in a completed physics, chemistry, and neurophysiology, and all there is to know about the causal and relational facts consequent upon all this." So for Armstrong and for others, the physical is to be defined over a completed physics, a physics in the end. But what is this final physics? The answer, as Hempel pointed out, is that we have no idea.

Basing one's notion of the physical on an unfathomable theory seems to be a serious enough problem to discourage defining the physical over a final theory. But most philosophers ignore this problem and charge ahead to the more juicy questions, such as whether there could be physical duplicates of us that are not conscious (the question discussed in an earlier chapter of whether "zombies" exist).

113

Here they face another serious consequence of using the notion of a completed physics to explain the physical: It allows for physicalism to be true even if the mind is not physical! For what is a completed physics? It would seem to be a physics that explains *everything*. But then, if dualism is true and the mind is not physical, it will explain this too. Physicalism, then, becomes trivially true—that is, since a true and complete theory of the world will explain everything, physicalism will also explain everything. And although there is nothing wrong with trivial truth *per se,* this is not the kind of solution to the mind-body problem most philosophers would accept. For neither physicalists nor their foes think that we already know by definition that the mind is physical.

A related problem exists for those who define the physical in terms of a final physics: Since we cannot predict the course of physics, we cannot be sure that a final physics will not include mental properties, qua mental, as fundamental properties. Yet, if final physics takes the mental realm to be fundamental, the difference dissolves between physicalists who claim that mental properties will be accounted for in final physics and dualists who claim that mental properties are fundamental.

The physicist Steven Weinberg has referred to the final theory as a set of principles that would, if achieved, bring to an end "the ancient search for those principles that cannot be explained in terms of deeper principles." Now this certainly has a nice ring to it, but I do not think it can help us formulate the debate over whether the mind is physical. For if we take the final theory to be the theory that will end our search for ultimate principles, and we take the physical to be either whatever is mentioned, as such, in the final theory, or can be explained by it, the mind could not but be physical. Certainly, either the ultimate principles will explain mental phenomena or they will not. And if they do, that means that the mind is something that can be explained in terms of the final theory; but even if they do not, then facts about the mind will themselves be fundamental principles and thus would be part of the final theory. So we are back, once again, to claiming that the mind is physical by definition. And as I've said, this is not what is intended by those who are on either side of the debate. It is beginning to seem that Hempel's dilemma is treacherous indeed.

Is there a solution to the body problem? I think there is, but it is not one that turns physicalism into a unified thesis. The solution is to merely define the physical negatively: The physical is the nonmental, or rather, the fundamentally physical is the fundamentally nonmental. What this says is that physicalism is true if everything ultimately depends upon nonmental phenomena. And whether the nonmental phenomena are captured by physics is a separate issue and has nothing to due with their physical respectability.

But physicalists are not only concerned about the status of the mind. They often have a host of other views about the world: There are no purely abstract entities; values and beauty are not fundamental features of the world; and so forth. Defining the physical negatively in terms of the nonmental does not obviously exclude these other realms. And physicalism, it is sometimes thought, should present a unified theory of the world that excludes all these phenomena in one fell swoop. I am skeptical about whether this can be done. Although I think that by understanding the physical in terms of the nonmental we can imbue meaning into the debate over whether the mental is physical, I'm afraid that the question of whether everything is physical, that is, the question of whether physicalism as a grand unified thesis of the nature of the world is true, falls by the wayside.

SUGGESTIONS FOR FURTHER READING

I present more in-depth arguments against many of the typical ways of understanding the physical in my paper "The Body Problem," published in the journal *Noûs* 33 (1999): 3. Some of my inspiration comes from Noam Chomsky's lovely short book *Language and Thought* (Moyer Bell, 1993) and Tim Crane and Hugh Mellor's aptly titled paper "There Is No Question of Physicalism," published in the journal *Mind* (1990): 99.

17

Ah, the Emotions

Like a skein of loose silk blown against a wall
She walks by the railing of a path in Kensington Gardens,
And she is dying piecemeal
of a sort of emotional anemia.
                    —EZRA POUND, "THE GARDEN" (1916)

O ur lives are filled with emotions. After a difficult interview, you
are offered the job of your dreams and you are brimming with
happiness. You are waiting to find out the results of an operation your
father just went through and you are beset with anxiety. You find out
that a childhood friend was killed in a car accident and you are
overcome with sorrow. Happiness, anxiety, sorrow, fear, contented-
ness, lust, rage, and jealousy are all part of our emotional landscape.

Perhaps some of us have never experienced certain emotions. For
example, there are those lucky few who claim to never have felt
jealousy. And it is likely that some mental states that we think of as
emotions are absent, or at least not named, in other cultures. For
example, perhaps the emotion referred to by the German word
Schadenfreude, which consists of pleasure derived from someone else's
misfortune, is present only in certain cultures. Other emotions, however, such as happiness, sadness, fear, and anger, are recognized by all
peoples.

Emotions are clearly important to our decisions—we pursue
actions because they make us happy, we avoid things we fear, we
marry out of love—yet just what they are is difficult to say. Let us

spend some time, then, thinking about these passions of the soul: our emotions.

The emotions resemble each other, as do the members of a family; and this family resemblance sets them apart from other aspects of our minds such as thoughts and sensations. But in what ways are the emotions different from thoughts and sensations? Do they require a unique analysis? Or can we understand them as combinations of other mental processes? For example, can we, as some philosophers have thought, explain all emotions in terms of beliefs and desires? Such an explanation might go as follows: When Sally is afraid of an approaching tiger, her fear is nothing more than her belief that there is a tiger approaching in addition to her desire to get away from the tiger. Similarly, Sally's being happy to receive a job offer might be described as consisting of her belief that the offer has been made and her desire to have the offer.

But though beliefs and desires typically are involved in emotions, this sort of account seems to leave out something important: that there is a certain sort of feeling we have when we are in an emotional state. Fear, for example, involves a characteristic feeling—the feeling, for lack of better terminology, of fear. However, one can believe that there is a tiger approaching and desire to get away from the tiger without feeling the fear at all.

So it seems that we need more than beliefs and desires to account for emotions; we need an account of what it feels like to be in an emotional state. Or at least we need such an account for those emotions that have characteristic feelings or sensations associated with them, and perhaps not all of them do. We speak of the heat of anger. But does anger literally feel hot? It sometimes does result in a rise in blood pressure with a concomitant reddening of the face. Anger, however, comes in a variety of styles, and some anger might be better described as cold or cool. Perhaps some anger might lack any feeling at all. For example, you might be so angry about something that you feel numb. Or can numbness itself count as a feeling? But even if all kinds of anger have associated sensory feelings, perhaps not all emotions come equipped in this way. Think about the emotions you have experienced today. Have they always had a sensory aspect?

What is the feeling of jealousy, or of love, or of shame? Certain sensory elements seem to be associated with these emotions, but the quality of the feeling or sensation is not always apparent. Identifying the feelings associated with emotions is especially difficult, since we can be mistaken about whether we are feeling a certain emotion. For example, Stan might not know that he is feeling resentment toward his spouse, Jennifer, for deciding to quit work and go to art school. After all, Stan has been encouraging Jennifer's artistic pursuits for many years, often mentioning that art school would be a good way for her to develop her natural talent. And he might feel that he is entirely behind her decision. Nonetheless, certain aspects of his behavior—for example, his staying later at work, shirking his household duties, and so forth—might reveal to Jennifer that, even though he is not aware of this, he actually resents her. And Stan might come to realize this as well.

This aspect of emotions—that one might have a certain emotion without realizing that one has it, stands in contrast to sensations. As we have mentioned in earlier chapters, although not all philosophers agree (and perhaps by this point in the book you have come to realize that there is precious little about which all philosophers agree), many think that we cannot be drastically mistaken about sensations, such as pain, pleasure, and feeling cold. For example, the feeling of pain, in contrast to the feeling of love or the feeling of resentment, is not something that goes unnoticed. If it honestly seems to me that I am not feeling pain, it makes little sense to say that someone else could correct me and point out that I really am in pain. Jennifer, however, is able to point out to Stan that he actually resents her.

So emotions seem to differ from sensations inasmuch as we can be drastically mistaken about the former but not the latter. Or even if we can be mistaken about sensations, the mistake is of a different sort, since even if it makes sense to say that you can have pain of which you are not aware, it seems that such pain could easily be brought to consciousness with a quick shift of focus, whereas unconscious emotions may not be apparent to their possessors even after they have tried to focus on them. Jennifer, for example, might have to argue for months before she is able to persuade Stan that what he feels is resentment.

Assuming that emotions have characteristic feelings, or sensory elements, we should ask how these characteristic feelings are related to the behaviors typically associated with the particular emotions. For example, extreme sadness is associated with crying, but what is the relationship between the sadness and the crying? Does a feeling of sadness cause crying? Or might crying cause sadness? Or could it be that something other than either the feeling of sadness or the crying causes both?

We typically think that certain feelings cause behavior, in this case, that the feeling of sadness causes the crying. However, the nineteenth-century philosopher William James denied this. He held, roughly, that when we come to know or perceive certain things, such as that a childhood friend has just died in a car accident, this causes certain physiological changes, such as crying, and that it is the physiological changes that cause the feelings, in this case, the crying that causes the feeling of sadness. James used the example of the emotion fear. What is it to be afraid of a bear? According to James, seeing a bear causes certain physiological changes in us: our hearts beat faster, we start to sweat, and we run away. The emotion of fear consists in recognizing these physiological changes; or in other words, it's not fear that causes us to run away but, rather, the running away (and other physiological changes) that causes the fear.

Do we have control over our emotions? Sometimes I feel annoyed and exasperated when the bus I take to work is late. I know that this particular bus is sometimes late and would like to be able to just accept this and not let it affect me emotionally. Is it possible for me to merely decide to not let the lateness of the bus bother me? I could decide to take a more reliable form of transportation, such as the ferry, so that I would not have this problem, and this might be a wise choice (though since I would still need to transfer to a local bus, it might not save any time). But can I remain in the same situation that tends to provoke my anger, and yet decide not to get angry? Perhaps to a certain degree I can. If I see that the anger is doing me no good, I can try to look at the situation differently and practice staying calm.

"Don't let it bother you" is advice we often hear, but how we go about not letting something bother us is not clear. We can recite the advice to ourselves over and over as a kind of mantra ("I won't let it bother me, won't let it bother me, won't let it bother me"), but does this help? Maybe it does, but often just a little.

What about love? Can we control with whom we fall in love? Again, saying mantras (such as "I will not fall in love with her, I will not fall in love with her") over and over usually accomplishes little. We all know individuals who are involved in what they themselves can identify as a "bad relationship." Just leave the person, we might say; and the response we often get is, "But I can't, because I'm in love with her." What is this binding factor of love that prevents people from doing what they know is in their own best interests—that pulls us like gravity to someone, whether or not that particular direction is best for us?

Of course, it might be that the trouble of a bad relationship comes not just from not being able to control your feeling of love, but also from not being able to control your actions. That is, what a person in a bad relationship might need to do is to take action and get out of the relationship despite the continued feeling of love. Thus, Warren may have no control over whether he loves Wendy, yet the trouble that results in their relationship may not be from the love, but from his not being able to leave Wendy.

But perhaps it is possible to control whether we feel love for someone. At least, some of my students have claimed that they are able to choose not to feel love for someone. And it may be that with love, as with anger, we can try to change our outlook. But perhaps other emotions are even more difficult to control. For example, do we have any control over fear? It is true that we can learn not to be afraid of something. Children who at first fear submerging their heads underwater will, with repeated practice, come to enjoy it. But this does not really seem to be a case of controlling an emotional reaction. Rather, it seems to be a case of practicing something long enough that one no longer reacts a certain way.

But if something truly frightening happens—a robber enters your apartment in the middle of the night, for example—it may not be possible to simply not be afraid. The feeling of being startled, if it is to count as an emotion, might seem similarly unyielding to our control. You are quietly reading in the living room when your roommate drops a glass. You are startled. Would it even make sense to say to yourself that you should have been more in control and not reacted in that way? I have been told, however, that martial arts students are taught that it is difficult but not impossible to control whether they are startled.

Whether or not we can control our emotions, they have an effect on all of us. But how do emotions affect us? In particular, to what extent are our actions determined by our emotions? Furthermore, to what extent should our actions be determined by our emotions?

We often think that emotions bias us, so are the best decisions made dispassionately? Certainly, we can all remember times when our emotions got in the way of proper behavior—when anger, say, caused us to knock over a glass, or jealousy caused us to make a rude remark about someone that, if we had been more level-headed, we would not have made. However, are we really better off relying solely on reason to decide what to do?

Interestingly enough, there is some evidence that shows that living by reason alone is a severe handicap, making one unable to make decisions at all. This evidence comes from patients who have brain damage in the frontal cortex, an area of the brain that is thought to underlie emotion. Such patients will make poor choices about what to do or, even worse, will not be able to choose at all. A classic example is the case of Phineas Gage (1823–1860). Gage, while working on a construction project on a railroad, had a three-foot-long, oneand-one-quarter-inch-diameter iron tamping rod pass through his skull, damaging much of his frontal cortex. Remarkably, he regained consciousness within minutes, and after a speedy and apparently complete recovery, he returned to work. But things were never the same. He was unable to complete a task and unable to hold down a job.

The neuroscientist Antonio Damasio takes Gage and similar cases to illustrate just how important our emotions are to our ability to make practical decisions. The situation of one of his patients is especially telling. This individual, though capable of logical reasoning, lacked emotional grounding and was unable to make the simplest everyday decisions. For example, when Damasio suggested to this patient that he come back for another appointment the following month on one of either of two days, the patient went into a long monologue on the advantages and disadvantages of each day, but even after half an hour was unable to come to any decision. Finally, Damasio suggested one of the two days, and the patient simply accepted it without further ado.

Damasio thinks that Descartes made a fundamental error when he famously claimed, "I think, therefore I am." The error is in ignoring the fact that it is the emotions, more than thought, that make us who we are. And in understanding the emotions, he thinks, we need to focus not only on the brain, but also on the body as a whole. For without the body, he thinks, there would be no emotions. As he says in his book *Descartes' Error,* "Were it not for the possibility of sensing body states that are inherently ordained to be painful or pleasurable, there would be no suffering or bliss, no longing or mercy, no tragedy or glory in the human condition."

SUGGESTIONS FOR FURTHER READING

William James first presented his surprising view that the emotions are reactions to physiological changes in our bodies in a paper entitled "What Is an Emotion?" in the journal *Mind* 9

(1884). Antonio Damasio, though in a different way, emphasizes the bodily aspects of the emotions as well in his highly readable book *Descartes' Error: Emotion, Reason, and the Human Brain* (HarperCollins, 2000).

18

Brain Transplants and Personal Identity

"In us you see the highest development; but there are
those of us who believe that there is yet another step—
that some time in the far future our race shall develop into
the super-thing—just brain. The incubus of legs and chelae
and vital organs will be removed. The future Kaldane will be
nothing but a great brain. Deaf, dumb, and blind it will
lie sealed in its buried vault far beneath the surface of
Barsoom—just a great, wonderful, beautiful brain with
nothing to distract it from eternal thought."

"You mean it will just lie there and think?"
cried Tara of Helium.

"Just that!" he exclaimed. "Could aught be more wonderful?"

"Yes," replied the girl, "I can think of a number of things
that would be infinitely more wonderful."

—EDGAR RICE BURROUGHS,
THE CHESSMEN OF MARS (1922)

Imagine that in the distant future neuroscientists have perfected organ
transplants, their crowning achievement being the brain transplant.
With this new technology, someone who had severe brain damage, due
to illness or injury, could be put on the waiting list for a new brain.

John is in such a position after a motorcycle accident. His situation is dire; he is in a deep coma, with no chance of recovery save for the possibility of a brain transplant. While John is in the hospital a brain becomes available; the twelve-hour operation proceeds forthwith, and after the usual recovery period for such operations, the patient opens his eyes and asks for a glass of water. The question, of course, is, who is the patient: Is it John, or is it the individual who donated the brain? In other words, is it best to describe such an operation as a brain transplant or a body transplant?

The question of whether John would still be John even with a new brain involves thinking about what makes a person the same person over time. People change in many respects over the course of their lives. A blond child might turn into a brunette adult. A soldier might return from war with a missing limb. The cells in one's body are constantly dying off and being replaced. Beliefs change, worldviews are developed, and so forth. But even though people change in all these ways, there is still a sense in which there is one person who is going through all the changes. Are there certain qualities that must endure in order for a person to remain the same individual throughout change? Would having one's brain replaced by someone else's turn John into a different person, or would he remain the same individual because his body (apart from the brain) continues?

In thinking about these questions it is useful to keep in mind the distinction between being the same individual over time and having the same characteristics or properties over time. In English there are two different notions of *same*. For example, when I say, "Sally took the same train to Boston as I did," what I am saying could mean either that Sally was on the very same train that I was on, that is, the 3:00 P.M. Acela express on March 14, 2006, or it could mean that she was on a 3:00 P.M. Acela express, but on a different day. This sort of ambiguity arises with the word *identical* as well. For example, when I say that Mary Ann Evans is identical to George Elliot, I mean that Mary Ann Evans and George Elliot are one and the same person, yet when I say that my computer is identical to Brian's, I mean merely that they are the same model.

To help distinguish these different uses of *identity* and *similarity,* philosophers have termed the first sense, that is, the sense in which Mary Ann Evans is identical to (or the same as) George Elliot, as "numerical identity" and the second sense, the sense in which my computer is identical to Brian's, as "qualitative identity." It is important to keep in mind that the question we are concerned with when we are wondering whether John is the same person after his brain transplant is whether he is numerically the same person.

Perhaps what we need in order to answer this question is more information about John's condition. Fortunately, it is visiting hours at the hospital, so we can ask John some questions. Let us imagine that the dialogue proceeds as follows:

PROF. M: Hello, uh, John. You are looking quite well considering all you've gone through.

JOHN: Could you please tell me who you are? I've been informed that I am supposed to be someone named "John"; however, no one has bothered yet to tell me who my visitors are, which makes things rather awkward.

PROF. M: Well, I was your philosophy professor during your senior year.

JOHN: Don't tell me I need to learn philosophy during rehab before they are willing to release me—philosophy is something I avoided at all costs during college ... or at least it is something Jack, the guy from whom I got the brain, avoided at all costs. It seems that rehab is going to be a lot of work, considering all the things I am going to need to remember.

PROF. M: Actually, John, do you really think you will be *remembering* the things that you knew before the accident? You can't remember things that you never knew.

JOHN: This sounds like one of those philosophical questions that I would really like to avoid. Whether or not it is called *memory* doesn't matter to me. All I know is that the physicians claim to be working on my memory during rehab. But truth be told, I'm skeptical that the rehab will be successful. From what I've learned about my former self, it seems that I will need to develop a wide range of interests in things that I have no interest in whatsoever. And, as I told the doctors, I refuse to become religious. The only thing that John, who I guess I am supposed to be, and Jack seem to have in common is that we both were reckless drivers, but while his accident destroyed his brain, mine destroyed my body.

If we were to encounter this sort of situation upon talking to John, we would be very inclined to see the operation as a failure, if the operation was thought to be an operation to save John. For it seems that John did not persist through the operation. John, it seems, did not have a brain transplant, but rather his donor, Jack, had a body transplant.

But what if the dialogue were very different?

JOHN: Hello, Professor Montero. It's so nice of you to visit after the operation.

PROF. M: But of course, I was concerned about your condition. And I have to admit to a bit of professional curiosity. I am surprised that you know who I am.

JOHN: Not only do I know who you are, but I also know that I took your senior seminar on personal identity where I wrote a paper arguing that brain transplants amount to death. It's funny how the new technology seems to have proved me wrong on this.

PROF. M: I must admit to being a bit confused myself, as I was expecting that you wouldn't recognize me or remember any events from the past.

JOHN: It is not really so strange. You are probably just not aware of what can be done by neuroscientists these days. I also used to think that a new brain would come with all new knowledge. That is, I thought that once one had a brain transfer, one would think in just the same way as the donor did. However, the latest advances in brain transplants allow for a rearrangement of the neurons in such a way that rather than merely transplanting someone else's brain as it is into a recipient's skull, the donor's brain is reprogrammed so that it acts like the recipient's former brain. Of course, this can only be done if there is a record of the recipient's thoughts. But fortunately, a few years ago a technique was developed that allows one's entire retinue of thoughts to be downloaded on a computer. Knowing that I was a reckless driver, as soon as I heard about this technique, I had it done, and I had just updated the data a few days before the accident.

If this dialogue represented John's situation, we would be very inclined to say that the person after the operation was numerically identical to the person before the operation. But why would we be so inclined? One thought is that it is not really the material brain that matters for the continuation of a person, but rather the information contained therein. As long as your memories, beliefs, hopes, and desires are more or less preserved—as long as there is what philosophers call "psychological continuity"—the person counts as you. And in this scenario, John, despite having a different brain, remains psychologically continuous with his former self; thus, if we accept that you remain who you are as long as your psychological states are preserved, John is still himself after the operation.

Okay, then, but what are we to say about the computer that was storing all of John's information? If psychological continuity suffices to preserve your identity, then right when this transfer of information occurs, John would somehow need to be both the computer and his bodily self. Assuming that the process of transferring psychological information is perfect, the computer will be psychologically continuous with John, as will the new brain that is programmed with all his information. But how can one thing be identical—that is, numerically identical—to more than one thing? Everything is itself and not anything else. John, clearly, at the time of the transfer is still just himself, that is, his bodily self and not the computer. So is there more to preserving selfhood than preserving psychological states?

Is it plausible that what matters to survival is not your psychological states but rather your bodily states, that is, that you will remain you as long as you have the same brain and body? Here is a thought experiment from Bernard Williams that might incline you to think that it is. Imagine being told that you will be given a drug that permanently will wipe out all your previous beliefs, thoughts, memories, and so forth. And if that weren't bad enough, after taking this drug, you will be tortured in a way that will involve extreme pain. This seems like bad news indeed, for not only is it tragic to lose one's beliefs, thoughts, memories, and so forth, but also the idea of being tortured afterward is abhorrent.

Now imagine that you are told that someone else will be given all your psychological states after the drug wipes them from your mind and that this person also will then be tortured. Are you just as upset about this person being tortured as you were about the person, housed in your body, but without your beliefs, thoughts, and memories, being tortured? Of course, torture is a horrible thing, and it is upsetting to hear that anyone has been or will be tortured. However, in the second case, where your psychological states are preserved in someone else's brain, do you have a sense that it will be you who is tortured? If not, and Bernard Williams thinks that we do not, it would seem that what matters in survival is survival of the brain and body, not a continuation of our psychological states.

Where does this leave us? It seems we have conflicting intuitions about what it takes to preserve our identities. When John had a brain transplant that gave him entirely new psychological states, he ceased being John. However, when his psychological states were preserved, he was still John. So there is some motivation to think that your psychological states make you who you are.

But there is also motivation to think that what makes you who you are is your brain and your body, since if you were told your brain and body would be tortured after all your psychological states were altered, you would not want this to happen. You would not want this to happen because you feel that it would be you who was being tortured.

Which view is correct? This is an important philosophical question. Fortunately, or perhaps unfortunately if you happen to also be a reckless driver, it is not a question that you or your loved ones, for practical purposes, will need to answer in the foreseeable future.

SUGGESTIONS FOR FURTHER READING

The anthology *Personal Identity,* edited by John Perry (University of California Press, 1975), contains a superb collection of both contemporary and historical papers on personal identity.

19

Freedom of the Will

A particle of matter cannot tell us that it does not feel the
law of attraction or repulsion and that that law is untrue, but
man, who is the subject of history, says plainly: I am free and
am therefore not subject to the law.

— LEO TOLSTOY,

WAR AND PEACE (1869)

We are part of a cosmic system. Free will is an illusion.
We are the children of Cause and Effect. We are the
Unalterable, the Irresistible, the Irresponsible, the Inevitable.
Where there are two desires in a man's heart he has no
choice between the two but must obey the strongest, there
being no such thing as free will in the composition of any
human being that ever lived.

— GEORGE BERNARD SHAW,

BACK TO METHUSELAH (1921)

It seems that right at this moment you are free to either continue
reading this book or close it and put it away. Of course, certain
factors may be relevant to your decision to either continue reading or
stop. For example, perhaps this chapter has been assigned for your
philosophy course that meets shortly and you will be quizzed on the
chapter's contents. Or perhaps you have borrowed this book from a
friend who needs it returned right now. Or perhaps you find the
topic so interesting that you feel compelled to keep reading. Or

perhaps you are bored to tears. Even worse, though fortunately highly unlikely, perhaps someone has you captive and has threatened to torture your loved ones if you do not continue reading. All these situations would motivate you to either continue reading or stop reading, but it seems that in each case, even in the last, you are still free to either continue reading or stop. It would be very unwise to stop reading if you knew that as a consequence your loved ones would be tortured. Nonetheless, it seems, you could make this choice. If this is true, at least some of your actions are free, or, in other words, you have free will.

From the inside, free will is virtually impossible to deny. It clearly feels to me that some of my actions are performed because I am choosing to do them and that if I had wanted to, I could have chosen not to. Moreover, many of our punitive practices seem to rest on the assumption that we have free will. For example, if a mother abandons her child because of serious postpartum depression, she might not be held accountable, since it is thought that she was not acting on her own free will. In general, treatment rather than punishment is advised for those who we think are not acting freely.

But our legal practices as well as what we know from the inside seem to conflict with what science tells us the world is like: According to the current scientific picture of the world, there is no room for our choices to determine the course of events. The laws of science are either strictly deterministic, telling us that given one set of events, another must happen with absolute certainty, or they are probabilistic, telling us that given one set of events, another must happen according to a certain probability. From the inside it feels like we have free will, but from the outside it seems that we can't have free will.

Let us go through this a bit more slowly. For you to have free will is for you to be able to choose among alternatives. You are at a café, and you can have either coffee or tea. You ponder the possibilities and opt for tea. If you had been hankering for coffee, however, you could have chosen coffee. If you have free will, either of these choices was genuinely possible. Of course, you might not have gotten tea even if you had chosen it. However, according to those who believe in free will, there was nothing in the prior state of the universe that determined the choice you made. If people have free will, the laws of physics cannot determine the movements of the mind.

According to the laws of physics, however, given the prior state of the universe, there is only one possible path for the universe to take. For example, right now, I have a cup of tea on the table, which I ordered about fifteen minutes ago. It seems entirely possible that I could have chosen coffee. But if the world is determined, it is impossible that instead of choosing tea I would have chosen coffee. If the world is determined, things couldn't have turned out differently from how they are. Yet for me to have free will is for me to have the ability to choose to do one thing or another, for there to be a sense in which I could have chosen coffee and, unless there were mitigating factors, for the world to have evolved accordingly. So free will seems incompatible with determinism.

One way to think about this incompatibility is to imagine that there is a being who knows all the laws of nature as well as the current state of all aspects of nature. If determinism is true, this being could predict every future state of the world exactly. But if humans have free will, then there could be no such being, since the actions that are the outcome of free decisions cannot be determined in advance based on the laws of nature and the current state of nature. Indeed, if we have free will, someone with a mischievous streak who was told the predictor's prediction in advance could falsify the prediction: "Ah ha, the predictor thinks that I will order tea; in that case, I'll just order coffee," thus showing that there could not be a perfect predictor. So free will is incompatible with a perfect predictor, yet it seems that if determinism is true, then a perfect predictor could, at least in principle, exist.

The idea of a perfect predictor was vividly expressed and defended by the Marquis de Laplace (1749–1827), a French mathematician and astronomer. Laplace argued that there could be an intellect that, knowing all the laws of nature and the positions of everything, could see everything that would happen in the future, or as Laplace puts it, "the future, just like the past, would be present before its eyes." Is such an intellect, or what is often called "Laplace's demon," possible? If it were, then determinism of the strongest kind would be true. But it seems unlikely that it is.

A number of questions might occur to you about the possibility of Laplace's demon. For example, would having the demon's knowledge alter the course of the universe so that the starting point of the prediction would change? The intellect would have to take itself into account and predict how the universe would evolve given that a being has just predicted the course of the universe. But then the intellect also would need to take into account what would evolve given that a being has just predicted what will follow from just predicting the course of the universe. Now the being is led into an infinite regress, since it would need to predict what follows from predicting, and what follows from that, and so forth, which makes you wonder how the prediction could ever be made at all.

Current physics also gives us reason to think that there could not be a perfect predictor. A principle in physics, the Heisenberg uncertainty principle, states that it is impossible to accurately measure both the momentum and position of a particle simultaneously. If this is so, Laplace's demon could not even begin the task of predicting, since the demon would not be able to know the complete exact state of the world from which the future is supposed to be determined.

According to current physics, at the most fundamental level of reality, the world does not proceed deterministically but, rather, is inherently random. For example, we can know the probability that a radioactive isotope will decay in a certain amount of time, but we cannot know with certainty when it will decay. Famously, Albert Einstein expressed his aversion to this idea with his quip, "God does not play dice." However, as far as we know, nature does play dice, or as the physicist Niels Bohr put it in his characteristically light-hearted manner, "prediction is difficult, especially the future." And if this is correct, the world is not determined.

A world with random events rules out Laplace's demon just as well as a world in which our wills are free. If there are certain events of the world that are random, there could not be a perfect predictor. If there are random events, no matter how much we know about the prior state of the world, we would not be able to predict precisely what the future state of the world would be like. Should this, then, provide some reassurance to those who believe in free will?

Unfortunately, it seems that it does not, since having outcomes determined randomly is not the same as having them occur because of one's choice. Random occurrences are not precisely predictable, but this does not make them free. Just imagine that at the café, your choice of coffee over tea depends on the barista's toss of a coin: heads for coffee, tails for tea. It is random whether the coin will land heads up or tails up, but your ordering whatever you end up ordering would not be something you freely choose to do. Now, take away the barista and make the principles of the world themselves random. Now your choice, it seems, depends on what randomly ends up happening, and such a world is not a world in which our wills are free.

So it seems that free will is incompatible both with determinism and with randomness. This means that if we believe in free will, we claim that some events in the world are neither determined nor random. The question is, just what sort of process could this be?

Not everyone, however, holds that free will is incompatible with the way current science tells us the events of the world progress. These philosophers, called "compatibilists," hold that all the events of the world are either determined or random, yet our wills are nonetheless free. How could this be? One argument for this view proceeds along the following lines. For my ordering tea to be a free action, it must have been possible that I could have ordered something other than tea. And even though the laws of physics are deterministic or probabilistic, it was possible for me to order something else: There were other options on the menu; I was not at that crazy café where a customer's order is determined by a toss of a coin; I had enough money with me to order something more expensive than tea; I'm not addicted to tea and so could have chosen something else; and so forth. So it seems that my choice was free—and that it was free regardless of whether determinism is true.

According to this version of compatibilism, we are free when we are not being constrained. And in the relevant sense of "being constrained," it seems that we often are not constrained. To take another example, think for a moment about whether you want to raise your arm right now or leave it by your side. It seems that you are free to do either. You would not be free if you were in a straightjacket or physically constrained in some other way so that you couldn't raise your arm (for example, if you were paralyzed or someone was giving you an enormous bear hug). According to the compatibilist, being free from such constraints is compatible with the world being entirely determined (or random, as the case may be).

Does compatibilism afford us a solution to the problem of free will? Is it really as simple as: Freedom involves being free from physical constraints such as paralysis or straightjackets, and this often occurs even given determinism, that is, even given that there is no other way things could have gone? It is not clear that we do have a solution to the problem of free will. Imagine that you are in a straightjacket and cannot raise your arms. Could you still choose to raise your arms? It is not clear that you could, since you might not be able to choose to do something that is impossible. Try it: Can you choose to fly right now? I don't seem to be able to do this.

Still, it would seem that if you are capable of normal thought while being in a straightjacket, your thoughts are free; for example, you could think about what you were going to do once you got out of that hideous jacket, or you could think about the lovely times you once enjoyed before being strapped in it. True freedom, some philosophers argue, involves being able to decide to think about one or another of these or countless other situations. And as long as you have this ability, it seems that even in a straightjacket, you would still feel that you have free will: They have taken away my ability to move, you might think to yourself, but they haven't taken away my will.

On the compatibilist position, the only sense in which you are free to choose to think about one thing rather than another is the sense in which there are no constraints on your thoughts, constraints such as being under the influence of drugs or powerful distractions that do not let you think. So, given that the compatibilist accepts determinism, it is not true that you could freely choose to think about the lovely time you had on your spring break. You are going to think whatever the world determines you to think even when your mind is free from physical constraints such as powerful drugs.

If determinism is true, there are no other thoughts you could have thought and no other actions you could have taken. Whatever occurred would be the only thing that could have occurred. Given this, it is not clear that compatibilists have shown how free will can be compatible with determinism. Of course, it might be that the type of freedom that is being advocated by the libertarians does not exist. And it also might be, as the contemporary philosopher Daniel Dennett puts it, that compatibilism "gives us the only type of freedom worth having." But nonetheless, if you think that at least your thoughts should be free to go either this way or that way, the idea that free will is merely freedom from constraints might not satisfy you.

Another idea is that free choice is compatible with determinism because being free involves, for example, being able to abstain from doing something that is harmful, like smoking, and being able to follow through with things that are beneficial to us, like eating wholesome foods. Humans are free, on this view, because we are not like animals and infants who merely act on their desires. Rather, inasmuch as we are free, we can reflect upon our desires and then decide whether or not to pursue them. When we do not do this, when we are in the grip of an addiction or a compulsion, for example, our freedom, it seems, is taken away.

The contrast between being driven by our desires as opposed to acting on our well-considered self-interest, like the contrast between being in a straightjacket or not, does capture an aspect of how we typically think of freedom. We do not feel free when we are acting on a compulsion, yet when we reflectively decide to act in a certain way, we do feel free. But again, one can ask whether this contrast gives us the core notion of freedom that we were trying to elucidate earlier, since if our reflective decision to either act on a desire or not is itself determined, then are we really free to act one way or another? Perhaps such radical freedom does not exist, but if it doesn't, we are left needing to make sense of how we can punish someone for actions that he or she was determined to perform, or praise someone for something that he or she had no choice about doing.

The puzzle of free will is an important topic in the philosophy of mind not only because to will something, or to choose something, is a mental process, but also because the existence of free will seems to pose a threat to physicalism. It is extremely difficult to see how a physical account of the mind could leave room for free will. If the mind is ultimately nothing more than physical processes, say, the complex movements of quarks and leptons, and physical processes are either determined or random, how can any of our choices be free?

Perhaps one way to look at things is to say that, even though we cannot see how this could be true now, free will somehow emerges out of deterministic neural process. An analogy might be that we know that there are deterministic laws that govern the movement of planets. Yet, if current microphysics is correct, we also know that planets are composed entirely of particles that behave not deterministically, but randomly. So a question arises: How do we get the deterministic behavior out of randomness? Perhaps determinism does emerge, but how? And similarly, perhaps free will emerges, but we don't know how.

Before we take this route, we need to look at what else might be affected by a free will. The mind, we typically think, affects the body and the world. My decision to choose tea led to my asking for tea, which led to someone making tea for me and bringing it to my table. And, presumably, my decision to order coffee would have led to a different chain of events. But now we have not only the mind forging a path that is neither deterministic nor random, but also the world proceeding along a path that is neither determined by the previous states of the world, nor is the outcome of a certain probability. So it is not just that we need to accept the mystery of how the mind could be free given that our brains function deterministically, but also how the world, apart from the mind, could proceed along a deterministic path even though it is affected by a mind that does not.

Of course, it is not just physicalists who would run into this problem if they were to accept free will. Dualists also think that the physical world is determined or random and thus need to explain how a nonphysical, free mind can affect a world that is not free. If teacups, light switches, arms, and so forth are all physical and thus all governed by either deterministic or random laws, there seems to be little room for free will (be it physical or not) to affect the world. Free choice could not, it seems, make it the case that tea is on the table rather than coffee. True freedom, it would seem, could only occur in the mind.

Given the difficulty of accepting free will, it might seem simpler to just deny that we have it and accept that there really is no alternative way the world could have turned out. What would it be like for you to really believe that physical laws determine your choices? Would you lose motivation to do anything at all? Or would you just continue doing everything as you did when you thought that your actions were up to you?

SUGGESTIONS FOR FURTHER READING

Peter van Inwagen vigorously argues for the incompatibility of free will and determinism, ultimately defending the view that we have free will. Daniel Dennett defends compatibilism in his punchy book *Elbow Room: The Varieties of Free Will Worth Having* (MIT Press, 1996).

20

Immortality of the Soul

Few persons feel any anxiety from the impossibility of determining at what precise period in the development of the individual, from the first trace of a minute germinal vesicle, man becomes an immortal being; and there is no greater cause for anxiety because the period cannot possibly be determined in the gradually ascending organic scale.
—CHARLES DARWIN,
THE DESCENT OF MAN (1831)

"The phenomena of life, Hump," he girded at me. "Stay and watch it. You may gather data on the immortality of the soul. Besides, you know, we can't hurt Johnson's soul. It's only the fleeting form we may demolish."
—JACK LONDON,
THE SEA WOLF (1904)

Eternity's a terrible thought. I mean, where's it all going to end?
—TOM STOPPARD,
ROSENCRANTZ AND GUILDENSTERN ARE DEAD (1967)

What would your life be like if you knew with absolute certainty that there is an afterlife? Would knowing that there is life after death enable you to go about your time on earth without the nagging feeling, mostly suppressed, though every once in a while rearing its head, that sooner than you would like, it will be all over? Would you live differently so as to attain nirvana in the hereafter? Or perhaps you already think you're doing your best (though it is the rare individual who actually is). Would you then be content knowing that you will be rewarded in the end? Or, as Fredrick Nietzsche (1844–1900) thought, would the idea of a blissful afterlife make you disenchanted with this life, as this life would seem to pale by comparison?

Of course, just saying that there is an afterlife does not tell us what this afterlife would be like. If we knew that in the afterlife we would be punished for bad deeds done in this life, we would likely have further motivation to avoid performing bad deeds. But perhaps the afterlife would not be one in which those who perform bad deeds here are punished. Perhaps the afterlife does not does discriminate between those who have been bad and those who have been good and provides everyone an equal opportunity to attain happiness.

Would the knowledge that there is an afterlife at all, even an equal opportunity afterlife, affect the way we live? Death would not be the end of it all. But it seems very anxiety-provoking to think that we will be leaving all that we love about this world and entering an unknown. In any event, many of us dearly want this life not to be the end. Given this, it is interesting to ask which philosophical views about the mind allow for an afterlife.

Dualists, that is, those who believe that the mind is distinct from the body, typically believe in an afterlife. But the theory of dualism does not imply that the mind or soul is immortal. That is, even if dualism is true, the soul might not be immortal. This point has sometimes been missed by even the greatest of philosophers. The seventeenth-century philosopher and mathematician Rene Descartes originally subtitled his masterpiece *The Meditations on First Philosophy*. In that text he argues that the mind is distinct from the body, "in which the existence of God and the Immortality of the Soul are demonstrated." He changed the subtitle to "In Which the Real Distinction between Mind and Body Is Demonstrated" when it was pointed out to him that, although he argued for the distinction between mind and body, nowhere in the book did he argue for the immortality of the soul. And the former does not imply the latter.

The mind may be separate from the body, yet it might be that whenever we undergo bodily death—what we now simply call death—our minds die as well. For example, it could be that although the mind is distinct from the body, bodily disease and deterioration eventually causes the mind to stop functioning or living. So dualism does not ensure that our minds will in some way survive bodily death.

Dualism, however, does allow for immortality. In the here and now, according to the dualist, the soul (or equivalently the mind) and the body are distinct entities that causally affect each other. But this connection, according to the dualist, could be broken, and the mind could continue to survive after the death of the body. Is there reason to believe any one of these views is true? As all our scientific knowledge of life and death is based on our earthly existence, science is silent on the topic. Perhaps science will evolve so as to be able to delve into questions about the afterlife. But for now, if you accept the immortality of the soul, you will need to find support for your view elsewhere.

There are a variety of ways that the mind, for the dualist, could continue on as a disembodied soul. The mind could be resurrected along with the body, or the mind could be reincarnated in a different body. However, how any of these could occur is rather mysterious. For a start, we should ask what exactly a disembodied mind is. Where would one be? Or might disembodied minds not be located anywhere? When a mind is connected to a body, we differentiate minds by the bodies to which they are connected, that is, mind a and mind b count as distinct minds when they are connected to distinct bodies. This is so even if mind a and mind b are psychological duplicates of each other, having the same beliefs, thoughts, feelings, wishes, desires, and so forth.

Disembodied minds, however, cannot be distinguished by their associated bodies. Thus it might seem that if disembodied minds a and b are psychological duplicates, a and b must be one and the same mind. But, intuitively, it seems that disembodied minds can count as different minds even if they have all the same psychological states.

The idea of resurrection also prompts various questions. For example, how could the mind be resurrected along with the body when the body is apparently buried beneath the earth and remains there until it decomposes? Likewise, the possibility of reincarnation raises questions. How does a soul attach to another body? Does it move in space so that it is located in someone else's body? If so, how does this occur?

Can one hold that the mind is entirely physical and consistently believe in immortality? Most physicalists deny immortality and rather believe that when the body ceases to function, there is nothing else; it is all over. However, it is not clear that this position is forced on them because of their physicalist views, for it seems that even if one is a physicalist, one can allow for certain types of immortality.

For example, if we can make sense of the idea of resurrection of the body, it would seem to allow for immortality even if we are entirely physical, for if we are our physical bodies, and resurrection is resurrection of the physical body, then a physicalist can accept resurrection. And along the lines of resurrection, but in a naturalistic vein, a physicalist might find immortality, that is, immortality of the body, in the idea that the matter of one's body, whether it decomposes in the earth or transforms into smoke and ashes upon cremation, remains here. Perhaps physicalists can even think of themselves as merely part of one giant ecosystem. At death, on this view, all that happens is that the part of the ecosystem that is you begins to serve a different function, for example, as worms' meat.

The idea of reincarnation is a bit more difficult to accept for a physicalist, but certain physicalist views might allow for it nonetheless. For example, if you are a physicalist who believes that the mind is the program of the brain, perhaps neuro/computer scientists in the distant future could take your mind's program and program another brain with it. That means that you—if you are the program of your brain—could be "reincarnated" in various brains or perhaps even in a computer. One wonders, of course, what would happen if your program were to be installed in more than one brain or computer at a time. Would there be two of you? Also, what would happen if your program were to be installed in a different individual while you were still alive? Would that other individual be you as well? We can avoid saying that you would be two or more people (or computers) by maintaining that you would survive as long as there was only one body or machine running the program. But if you were just your program, why would you cease to be your program when your program was installed more than once?

Although resurrection and reincarnation may be possible within physicalism, very few physicalists accept them. However, two other ideas of how we may survive after our bodily deaths could be attractive to physicalists. One involves genetic immortality. Physicalists sometimes find solace in the idea that in having children, you pass on your genes, since your children will likely have fifty percent of your genes. Your genes, which in at least one sense are what makes you who you are, live on to some degree in your children. This does seem to be a sort of life after death, but it is not an everlasting one. Over each successive generation, your genes dissipate; your great-great-great-grandchildren probably will not significantly resemble you either physically or mentally.

Perhaps a better physicalist means of immortality is in the persistence of what the contemporary evolutionary biologist Richard Dawkins calls our "memes." While genes transmit biological information, memes, according to Dawkins, transmit cultural information. Similar to genes, the memes that stick around have survival value: Beethoven's fifth symphony is a meme, as is designer bottled water. Although memes are ideas, they need not be nonphysical ideas. And perhaps physicalists can feel a sense of immortality if one has lasting ideas. Of course, you do not need to be a physicalist to hope for immortality of your memes; what you need to do is write a great novel, think up a memorable tune, answer one of the big open questions in math, or perhaps solve the mind-body problem.

SUGGESTIONS FOR FURTHER READING

Dawkins presents his theory of memes in his provocative book *The Selfish Gene* (Oxford University Press, 1976), and John Perry's *A Dialogue on Personal Identity and Immortality* (Hackett Publishing, 1978) will keep you thinking about these issues until eternity.